graphic design for architects

design
Malcolm Frost
digital artwork
Newnorth Printing
pre-press
Mission Productions Limited
printing
Everbest Printing Co. Ltd., Hong Kong/China

ISBN 1 87690 772 X
Reference number 453

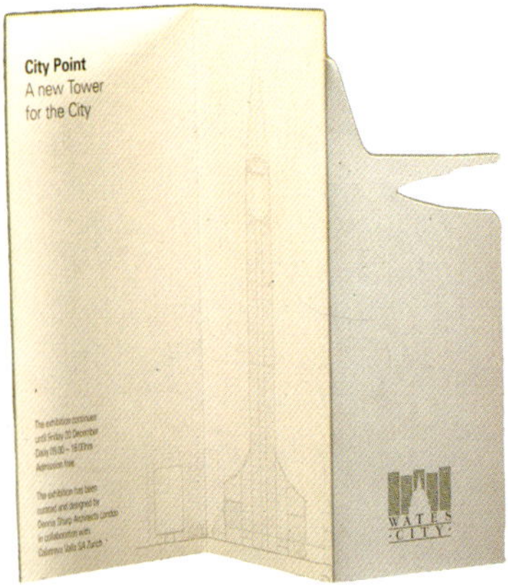

images

Commonwealth
Association
Of Architects

The Images Publishing Group Pty Ltd
Images House
6 Bastow Place
Mulgrave
Victoria 3170
Australia

telephone
(613) 9561 5544
facsimile
(613) 9561 4860
e-mail
books@images.com.au
internet
www.imagespublishinggroup.com

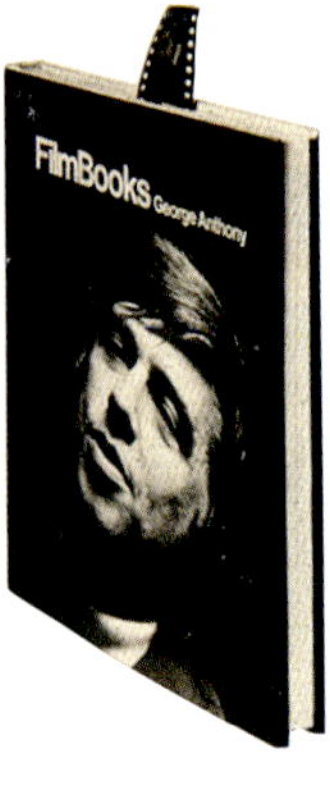

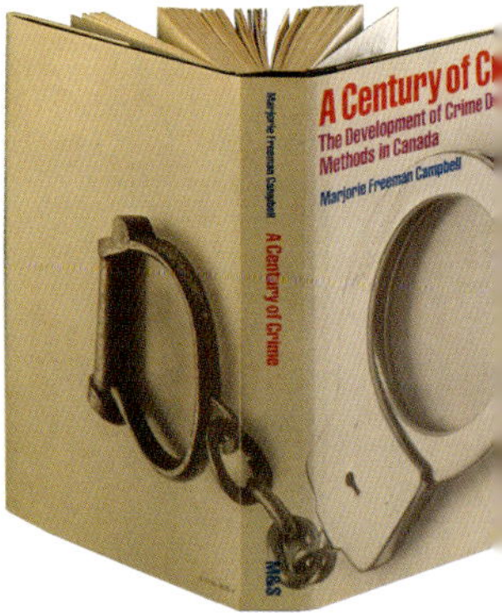

BROADWAY HIT!
COMING
direct from
THE LONDON PALLADIUM SHOW
PROMISES, PROMISES
book by NEIL SIMON
music by BURT BACHARACH
from NEW YORK
COMPANY
Mary
BEST MUSICAL 1970
A NEW MUSICAL

S N U G

Queen Anne's Aviary

The offices of the *Architectural Press* in Queen Anne's Gate were a sort of rookery made out of a small early eighteenth century terrace which had originally been professional chambers for lawyers who got private Bills through Parliament just down the road. So, of course, the whole building became a strange, confusing, delightful three-dimensional lattice of studies, each different from its neighbour.

Underneath was the source of inspiration, the Bride of Denmark, the amazing picturesque private pub created by the eccentric director H de C Hastings and friends Hugh Casson and John Piper from fragments of bombed Victorian boozers rescued after the Blitz. Everyone came there to gossip, not least because, on the slightest of pretexts, we could have it opened so we could serve guests, and (because of the licensing laws) drinks had to be given away.

Luckily, a few years before the end of our time in Queen Anne's Gate, I persuaded the management to give *The Architectural Review* editorial team a small set of rooms right at the top of the buildings, where we were free of the bustle of the weekly *The Architects' Journal,* and some distance from the endless haggling of the advertising department. Here, we became a mixed menagerie above the twittering, often raucous flocks of sparrows, starlings and swallows (with sometimes a vulture and a coot) that occupied the lower floors. Our changing team included ducks, thrushes, cockatoos, lyrebirds and the occasional flamingo or falcon. I tried to be a buzzard but did little except reproduce the creature's harsh cries.

Bill Slack, the art editor, was our Great Auk. He had coped with the erratic and often grossly inefficient behaviour of generations of editors, and continued the *AR's* tradition of being an imaginative, thoughtfully original magazine, visually as well as intellectually. But he was starting to become unwell, just as the magazine was beginning to become profitable and bigger. He needed help.

So we hired a heron, Malcolm Frost. His tall thin fastidious presence, his amazingly rapid verbal ripostes, and elegant typographical approach had a very quick impact on the magazine. While Bill sometimes tended towards the Baroque, Malcolm was Bauhaus. The interaction of the two sensitivities made the magazine visually lively and combative as it has always needed to be.

When Bill retired, Malcolm became art editor, and his calm, clear and sometimes dramatic approach still influences us today. We were bought by barbarians whose master was a swindler, and we had to leave Queen Anne's Gate. Our new quarters did not suit any of us, but least of all Malcolm. Curiously, after living in very small spaces, we felt that open plan was terribly confining. The heron spread his wings and flew away.

Peter Davey London | 10 | 2001

Malcolm Frost was born on Wednesday at 8.45am on the 3rd of July 1940 in South London. His father was a solicitor and his mother a professional dressmaker. He was brought up living in Pullman Court; attended Christ Church Primary School and Battersea Grammar. He studied design at The London School of Printing.

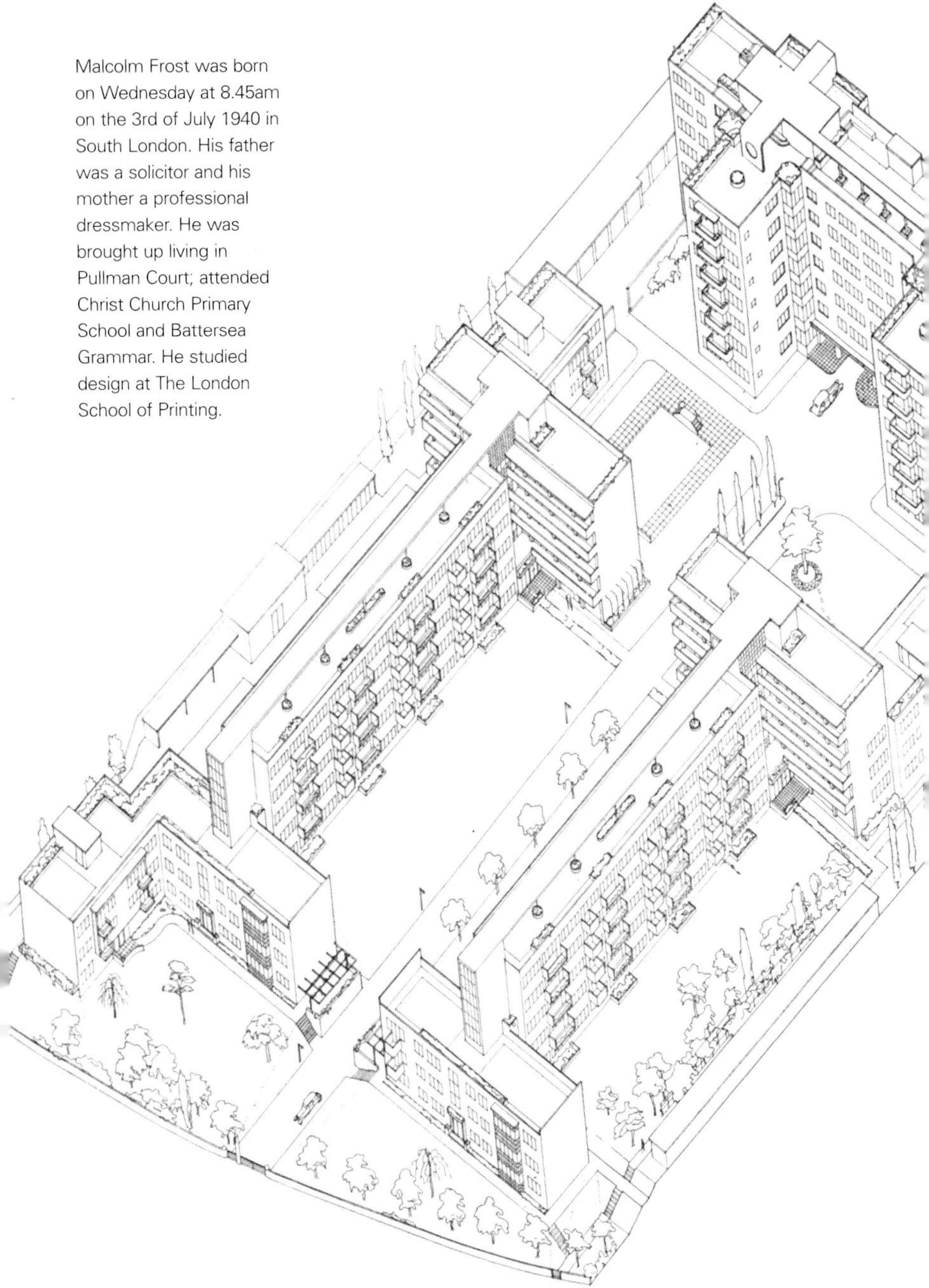

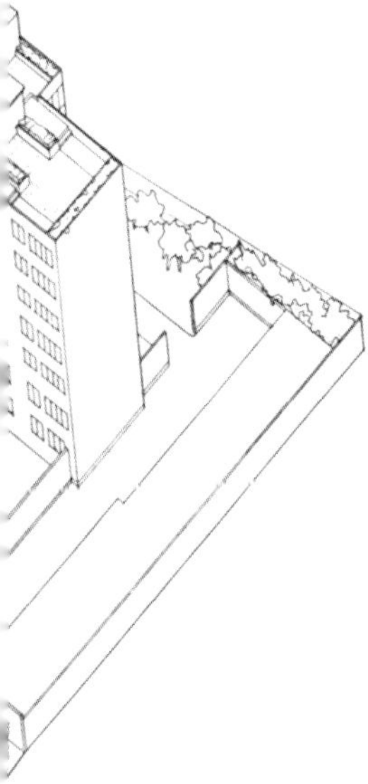

From a *Guide to Architecture of London – Seven Dials 2000:*
One of the most lively early modern designs in London. Pullman Court confidently combines the best of the lightness and picturesqueness of modern architecture for the progressive middle classes. The ensemble brings the air of a Mediterranean holiday resort to Streatham.

Frederick Gibberd
Pullman Court
1935

John Summerson for *The Architects' Journal –* January 1929:
James Wild at Streatham had already employed bricks of three colours to decorate the exterior of his church, before Butterfield's famous church in Margaret Street, and had continued to give style and character to the design in the use of ingenious devices.

James Wild
Christ Church
1840–42

Didya gota school tado this?

Derek Birdsall hired Frost to make the cover drawing above for Pelican Books 1960 – Frost's first published work.

I first met Malcolm Frost (everyone called him Jack then and I still do) forty-four years ago in a gloomy studio on the fourth floor of The London School of Printing in Back Hill, Clerkenwell. The building was a converted printing works, erstwhile home of *The Daily Mirror* and the cheeky weekly, *Reveille*.

The floors were concrete, the stairs bleak and unforgiving (no lifts in those spartan days) but the atmosphere was stimulating and exciting.

Frost came to the LSP from the constraints of a traditional grammar school in Streatham, South London, and thrived in the liberating atmosphere of the place supported and encouraged by Tom Eckersley, the newly appointed Head of Department.

Frost and I became friends early on and shared an interest in jazz and some of the things that made us laugh and made us angry. Our group was a pretty mixed bunch, mostly male, from a variety of backgrounds united in our ignorance of graphic design and an eagerness to fathom its secrets. The familiar expression for graphic design was 'commercial art' with its tired associations with Ashley Havinden posters and scraperboard illustrations of pipe smokers in ads in *The Radio Times*.

The LSP had a team of young lecturers and tutors such as Derek Birdsall, whose intelligence and enthusiasm fired us all, and active freelance designers like Ian Bradbury, Robin Fior, Richard Hollis, and LSP graduate Ivan Dodd. One of the full-timers was George Adams, a man at the genesis of modern graphic design as a student at the Dessau Bauhaus. Our History of Printing lecturer was the legendary HC (Harry) Beck, creator of one of the icons of British 20th century graphic design, the London Underground map.

We were young and impressionable back then. There were exciting changes happening in the creative arts in the late 50s. Frost and I shared some heroes – we relished the work of Milton Glaser, the film titles of Saul Bass; the ideas of Bob Gill; the creative sparks that flew from Doyle Dane Bernbach in New York; the typography of Armin Hoffman, Tom Geismar and Jan Tschichold; the cartoons of Ffeiffer and Andre Francois; and the music of Gerry Mulligan and Miles Davis. Frost became an early Bob Dylan fan, was seduced by Kerouac, Salinger and Aldous Huxley, and developed a lasting affection for the work of Ben Shahn.

In 1960 our little band of hopefuls dispersed, and whilst most of us found work in London, some were drawn overseas – Chris Whittaker to Canada, Derek Watson to Australia, the enigmatic Terry Smith to Germany, Ray Kyne to his native Dublin. And armed with his National Diploma in Design (Nothing Doing Diploma as cynics called it) and the Harold Nelson Prize for Outstanding Work in Line Drawing, Frost went to Oslo for a year where he worked for the advertising agency Alfsen and Becker. In 1962 he worked with DMA Design, a group of Soho-based designers and architects, mainly concerned with architectural products, with connections with *The Architectural Press.* In 1964 he joined Hans Schleger's studio, Schleger a seminal figure in British graphics, hugely influenced and disciplined his work. Later, Frost collaborated with Bob Gill to produce the 1968 *D&AD Annual.*

Some of Frost's work illustrated in this book comes from his time in Toronto where he spent five years as a director of Design Workshop, concerned with graphics and 3D. He returned to England in 1976 to work on a variety of freelance commissions before joining The British Council. After a period of 12 months, he left to teach at Coventry Polytechnic and later Limerick School of Art and Design in Ireland.

It was during his two years at *The Architectural Review* from 1989 to 1991 that he developed a special interest in graphic design for architecture. This led to his long-term collaboration with architect, author and historian Dennis Sharp with whom he designed books, posters and other material with architectural content. An important exhibition was held in London in October 2000 to celebrate 10 years of this successful partnership.

Frost remains a true individual – a free spirit. He is warmhearted and compassionate, outspoken and funny. He is a sharp critic of pretentiousness and dislikes the pernicious influence of fickle, fashionable trends in design. Some may find him stubborn as he clutches tenaciously to his faithful Rapidograph and type depth scale while deriding the pervasive AppleMac.

Today's designers are part of a much bigger industry than the one that greeted us in 1960 when we left the LSP. There is more competition, there are more influences and there are computers. We have all become aware that with smarter computers come more quick-fix graphics often achieved by people with little design training. Graphic design makes an important contribution to our lives, and increasingly we look to people like Frost to maintain its traditions. He remains committed to the principles of our LSP days, still convinced of the aesthetic of classical modern-movement work. Considering the technological changes our industry has embraced, good design still retains its universal importance.

The idea that the work of an individual, through a combination of inter-dependent trades, can communicate to thousands is very powerful. This belief is clearly demonstrated in the examples of the work shown in this book.

John Solloway London | 6 | 2001

The title of this introduction comes from the film *Heat* in which the character played by Robert de Niro picks up a sassy graphic designer in a bar and asks her about her work.

professional career

1960
Alfsen & Becker, Oslo, Norway
1962
Peter Hatch Partnership, London
1963
DMA Design, London
1964
Hans Schleger Associates, London
1968
D&AD, London – with Bob Gill
1968
Thames TV, London
1969
Design Workshop Inc, Canada
1976
Gillinson Barnett, Leeds
1978
Racal-Decca, London & Surrey
1981
The British Council, London
1989
The Architectural Review, London
May 1991
Freelance, London

NINE2NINE PHARMACY

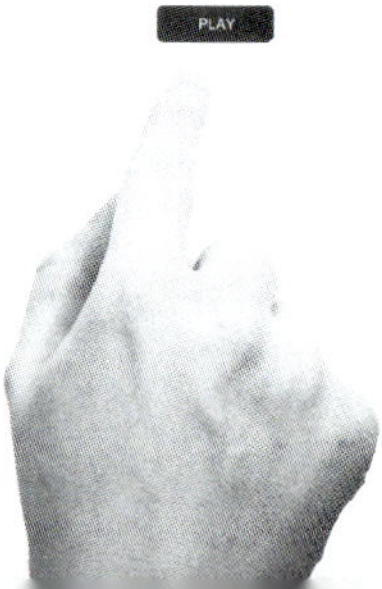

Young August
L'août Fou

with special thanks
Elsa Tatterka
Derek Farndell
Tom Eckersley
Derek Birdsall
Ian Bradbury
Ivan Dodd
Christine Hall
Terry Smith
Ben Shahn
Per Eggen
Injeborg Rorhus
Olav Angell
Tommy Heron
Geoff White
Ken Young
Hans Schleger
Pat Schleger
Robin Dodd
Bob Gill
Mike Harvey
Mick Loftus
Nick Milton
Mary Orchard
Andy Winterburn
Ken Knight
Barry Bracken
Brian Thompson
John Solloway
Rosemary Hood
Gordon Rookledge
Alison Kiteley
Graínne Egan
Peter Davey
Bill Slack
Dennis Sharp
Santiago Calatrava
Manfredi Nicoletti
Giulia Falconi
Keith Burgess
Paul Latham
Paul Jellis
Fiona Lafferty
Alessina Brooks
Kisho Kurokawa
Mahesh Patel
Rodney Harrigan
Andrew Scoones

for Slessor my dearest friend. Roma 2002.

Studio Downie Architects. London 1998.

 Catherine Slessor. London 1991.

Canadian funiture importer. Toronto 1974.

RIBA AIJ 1996

新進気鋭の
日本の建築家たち

EXHIBITION 25.3 – 16.4

 Emerging Japanese architects. London 1996.

Building
with
Light

Architectural photography book series. London 1995.

Commonwealth
Association
Of Architects

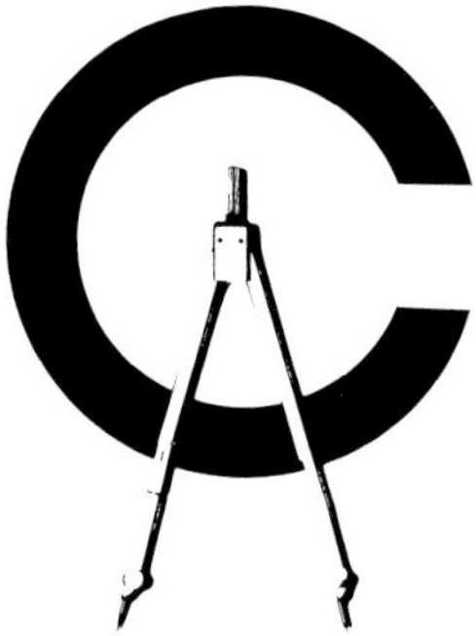

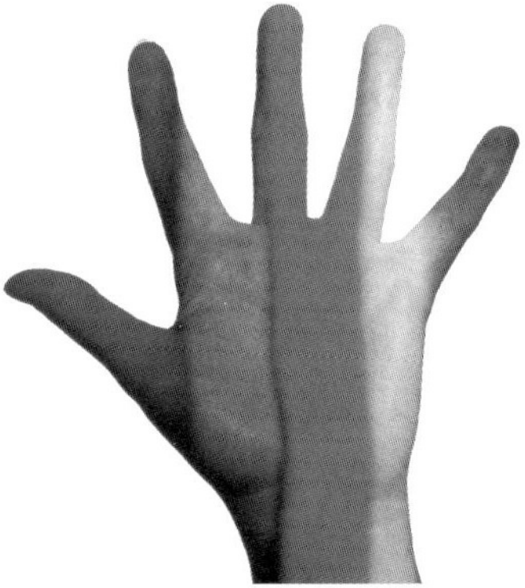

22 Commonwealth Association of Architects. London 1994.

 Design partnership. Toronto 1970.

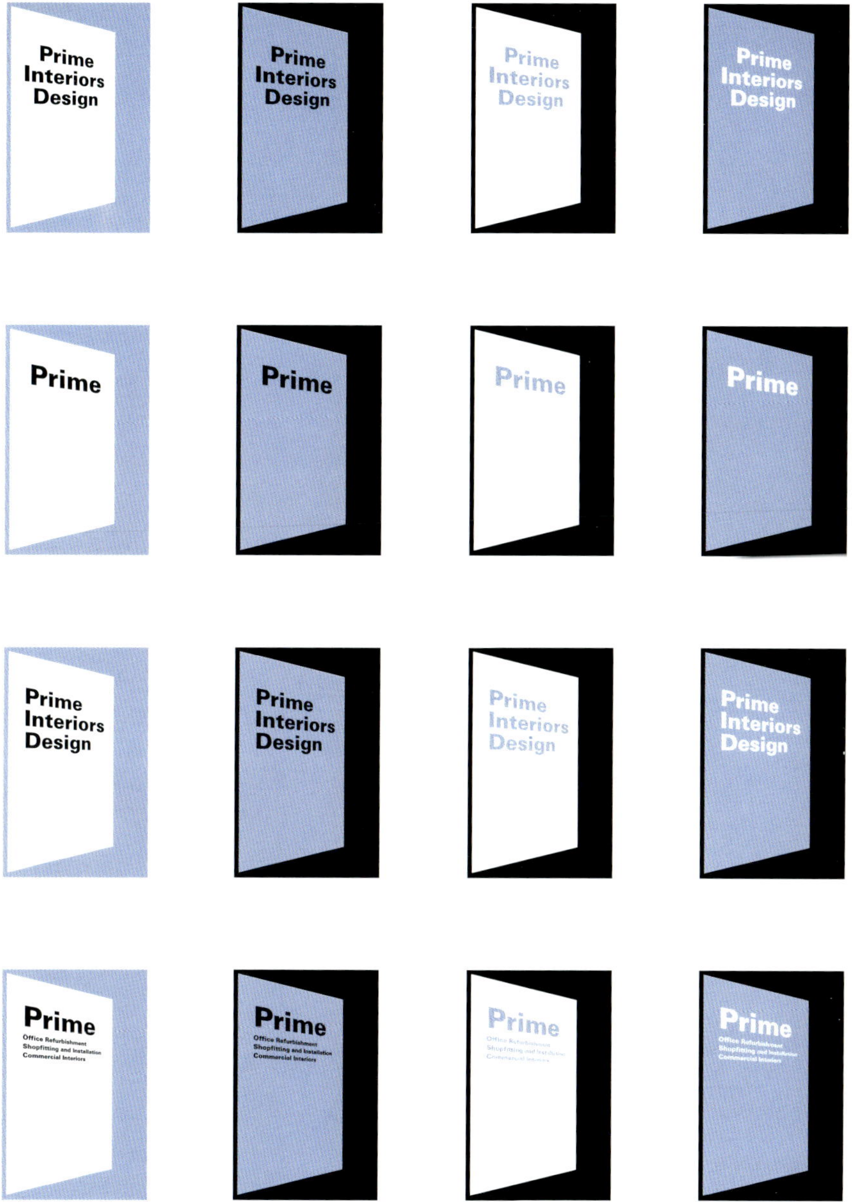

Prime Interiors Design. London 2002.

Design Brief

 Sarema Press. London 1984.

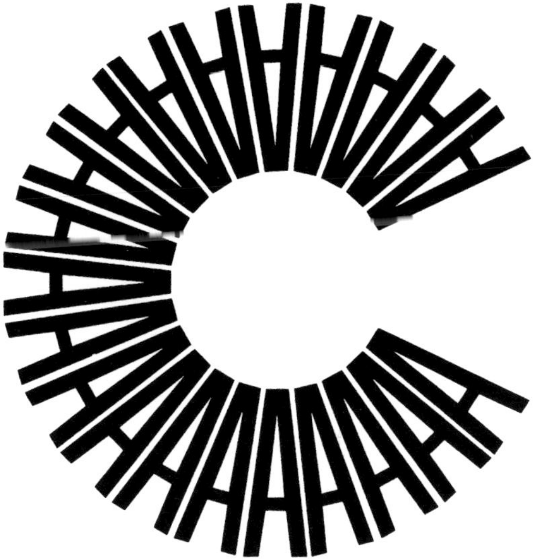

Association of Consultant Architects. London 1993.

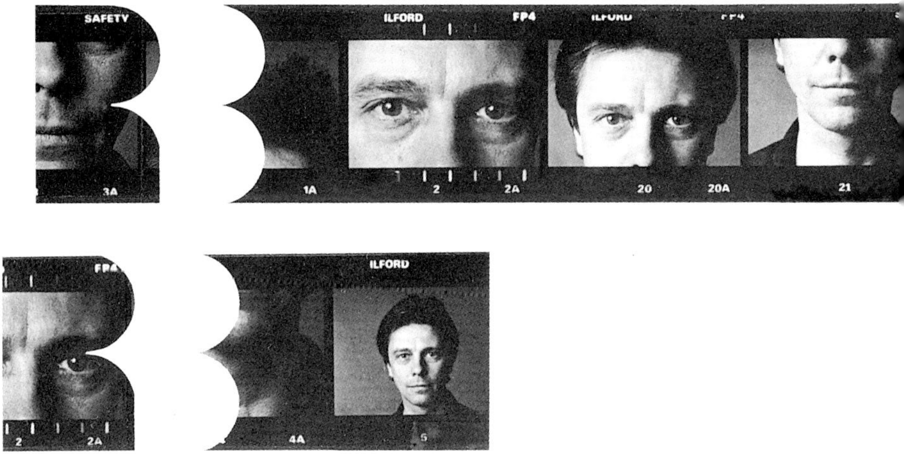

28 Rowan Bulmer architectural photographer. Leeds 1983.

International design exchange. Toronto 1972.

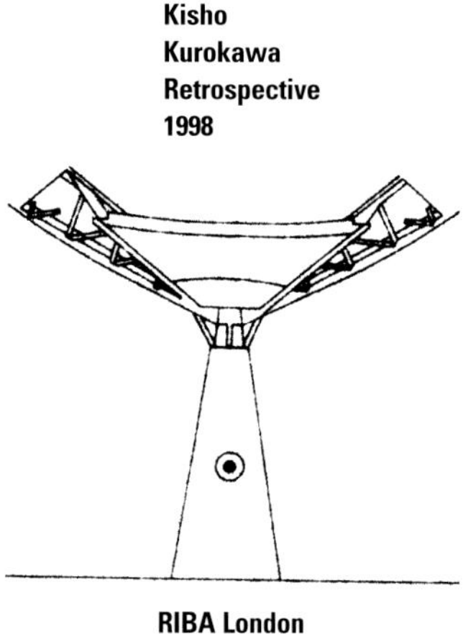

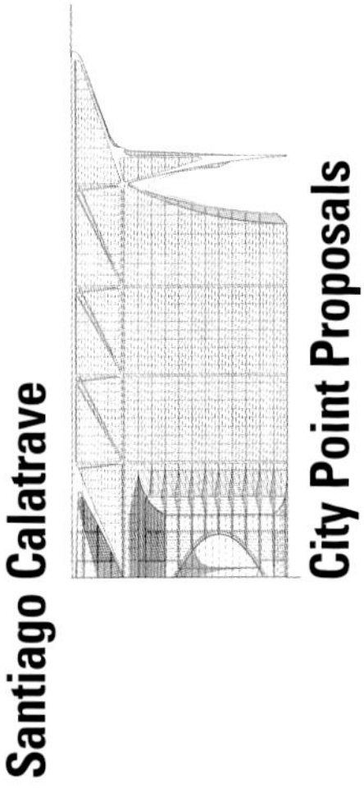

 Exhibition devices. Kurokawa. London 1998 | Calatrava. London 1998.

Exhibition devices. The Building Centre Trust. London 2000.

Dennis Sharp Architects

 Dennis Sharp Architects. London 1997.

Oscar Niemeyer
Royal Gold Medallist 1998
Gallery One
October 6-31 1998
RIBA Architecture Centre
Royal Institute of British Architects
66 Portland Place
London W1N 4AD
Telephone 0171 307 3699
Opening times
Monday, Wednesday, Friday and Saturday
08.00-18.00
Tuesday and Thursday
08.00-21.00
Admission free
Sponsored by
PREFEITURA
DA CIDADE DO RIO DE JANEIRO

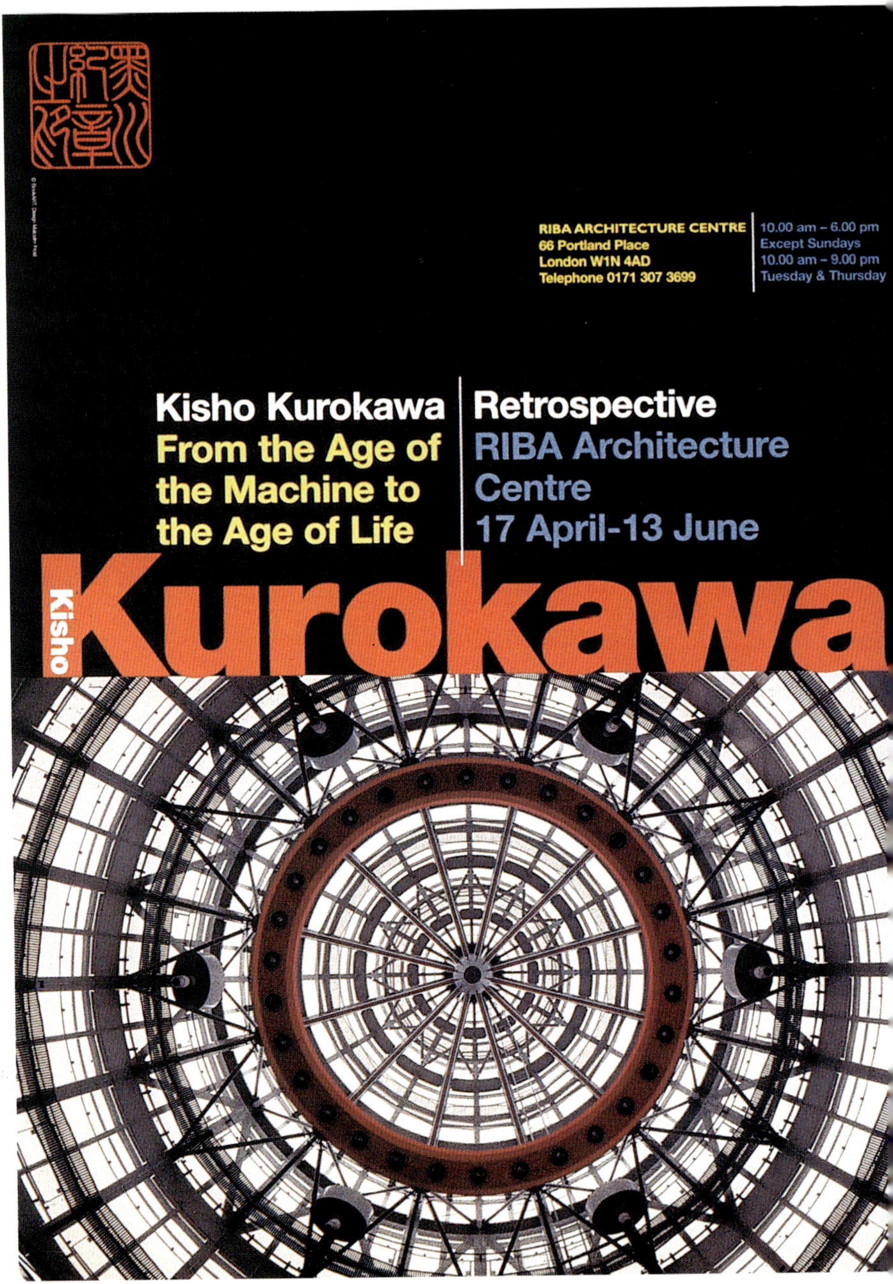
RIBA ARCHITECTURE CENTRE
66 Portland Place
London W1N 4AD
Telephone 0171 307 3699
10.00 am – 6.00 pm
Except Sundays
10.00 am – 9.00 pm
Tuesday & Thursday
Kisho Kurokawa
From the Age of the Machine to the Age of Life
Retrospective
RIBA Architecture Centre
17 April-13 June
Kisho
Kurokawa

Kisho Kurokawa. London 1998.

Poster with booking details. London 1993.

 Manfredi Nicoletti. London 1999.

Santiago Calatrava. London 1992.

Models
Building Centre
Exhibitions
1999 – 2000
Sport
18 November to 13 January 2000
Featuring
British Racing Drivers' Club
Cardiff Millennium Stadium
HOK + Lobb
Coventry FC Arena
Grandstand, Lords
Nicholas Grimshaw & Partners
Indoor Cricket School, Lords
David Morley Architects
Manchester Commonwealth Stadium
Arup Associates
Media Centre, Lords
Future Systems
SPORT

The Museum of Scotland
Edinburgh
Benson + Forsyth
Architects
The Building Centre
Trust Gallery
Object Integration
Models

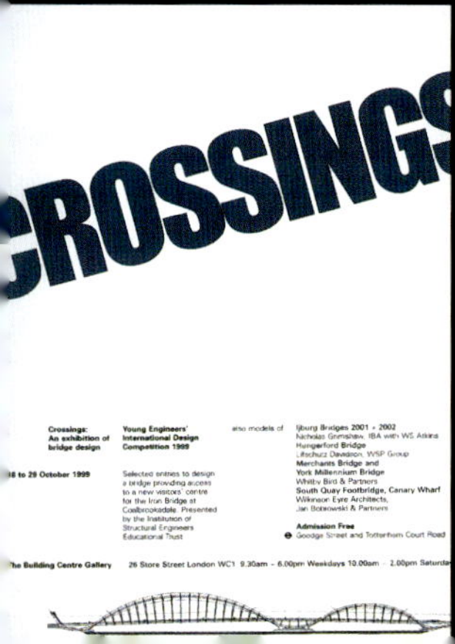

CROSSINGS
Crossings:
An exhibition of bridge design
Young Engineers' International Design Competition 1999
also models of
Ijburg Bridges 2001 - 2002
Nicholas Grimshaw, IBA with WS Atkins
Hungerford Bridge
Lifschutz Davidson, WSP Group
Merchants Bridge and
York Millennium Bridge
Whitby Bird & Partners
South Quay Footbridge, Canary Wharf
Wilkinson Eyre Architects,
Jan Bobrowski & Partners
18 to 29 October 1999
Selected entries to design a bridge providing access to a new visitors' centre for the Iron Bridge at Coalbrookdale. Presented by the Institution of Structural Engineers Educational Trust
Admission Free
Goodge Street and Tottenham Court Road
The Building Centre Gallery
26 Store Street London WC1 9.30am - 6.00pm Weekdays 10.00am - 2.00pm Saturda

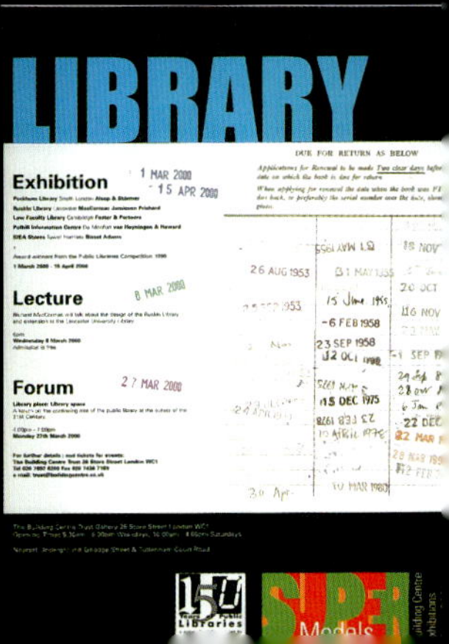

LIBRARY
DUE FOR RETURN AS BELOW
Exhibition
1 MAR 2000
15 APR 2000
Lecture
8 MAR 2000
Forum
27 MAR 2000
Library place: Library space

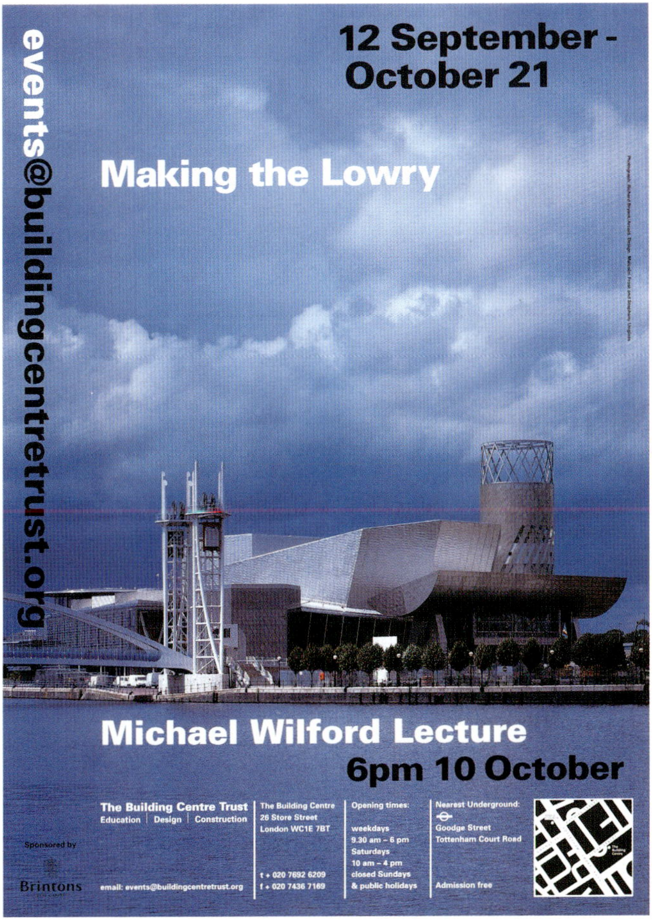

Five posters for The Building Centre Trust. London 2000.

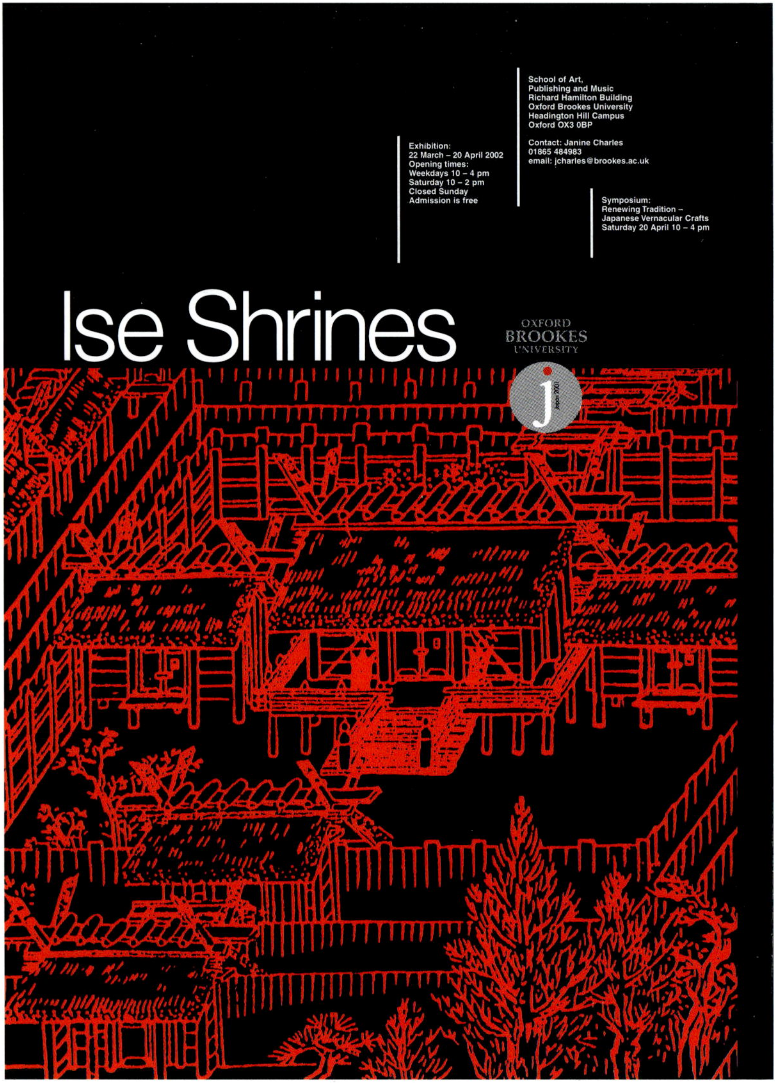

 Oxford Brookes University. London 2002.

Instruments of
Modernity :
Albert Frey
Harris Armstrong
Richard Neutra
Exhibition at
The Building Centre
Store Street, London
21 February until
11 March 1995
Weekends 9.30 – 17.15
Saturdays 10.00 – 13.00
admission free
Exhibition curator:
Stephen Leet, Visiting
Assistant Professor,
Washington University
School of Architecture
Organised by:
Washington University
School of Architecture
in conjunction with
DoCoMoMo US

Paul Rudolph–
American architect–
Legendary draftsman–
Inspired teacher–
24 January – 19 February 2000
The Building Centre Trust
Gallery: 26 Store Street
London WC1E 7BT
Weekdays 9.30am - 6.00pm
Saturdays 10.00am - 2.00pm
Admission free
Nearest Undergrounds -
Goodge Street and
Tottenham Court Road
An exhibition of Rudolph's work- 1940-1997
from Florida, New York, Texas, Japan,
Indonesia, Hong Kong and Singapore.
Anthony Monk curator of the exhibition
will present a lecture on Rudolph at 6.00pm on –
Tuesday 1 February details T0171 692 6209
Paul Rudolph was fired by
a passion for architecture -
and no effort was spared to
improve the quality in his
own buildings, or by inspiration
in the work of his students.
Norman Foster: A Paul Rudolph student | Yale University '61
Rudolph
Paul Rudolph 1918-1997

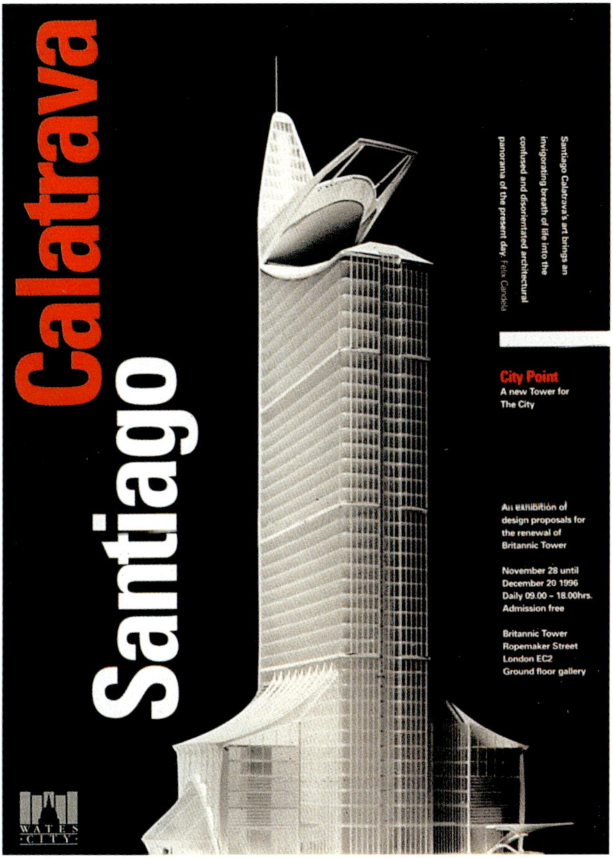

Paul Rudolph. London 2000.

Santiago Calatrava. London 1996.

 Paolo Rosselli. London 2000.

Santiago Calatrava. London 1992.

Felix Candela. London 1992.

Patron: HRH The Prince of Wales

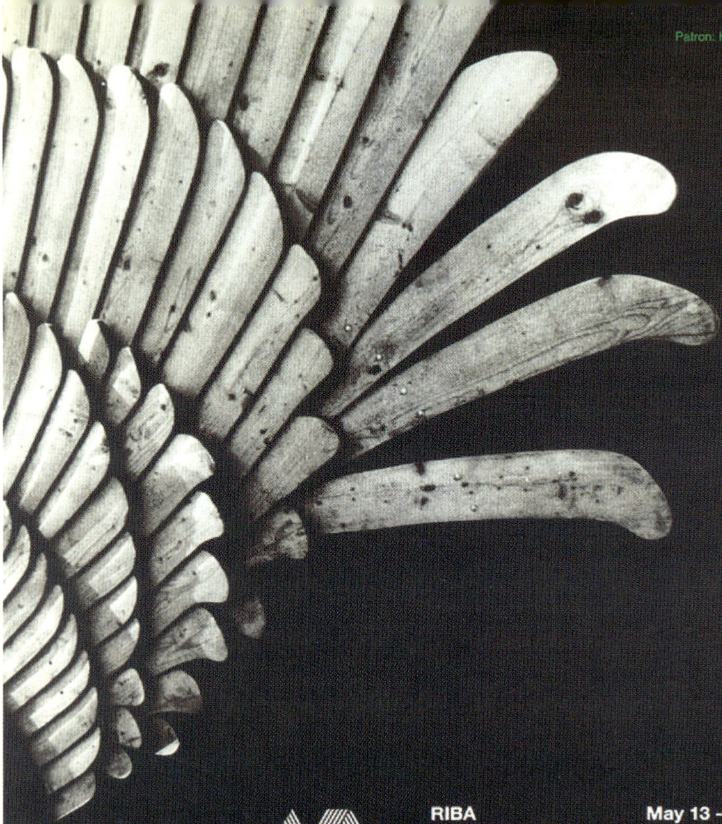

VISITING ARTS

RIBA
Architecture Centre
66 Portland Place
London
W1N 4AD

May 13 - June 12 1994
Mon to Fri: 10.00 - 17.30
Saturdays: 10.00 - 13.00

Admission Free

1994 DSA/BOOKART

IMRE MAKOVECZ

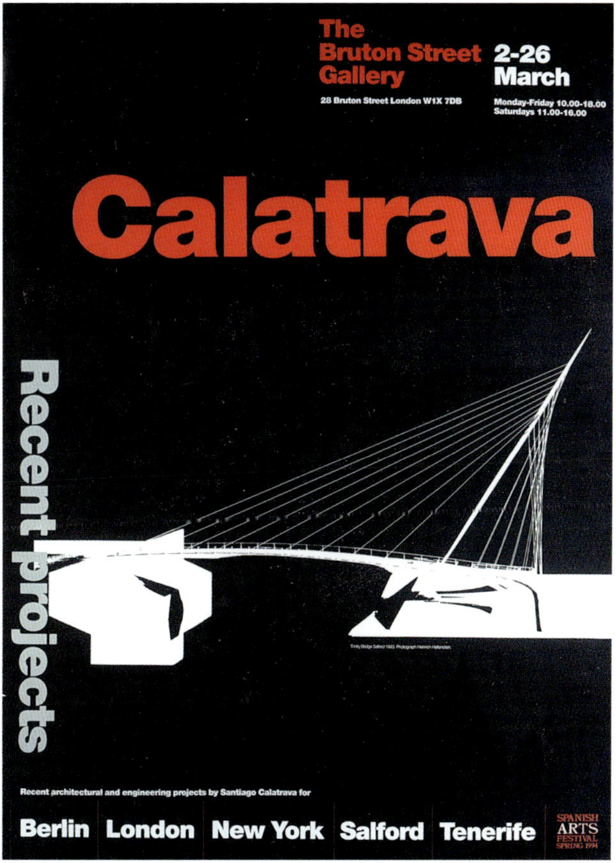

Imre Makovecz. London 1996.

Santiago Calatrava. London 1994.

 Kisho Kurokawa. London 2002.

Important in terms of Finland's need to increase exports and tourism was the completion in 1947 of Erik Lindroos's new factory for the Arabia Company.[47] Arabia is the main producer of ceramic products in Finland and its products range from sanitary ware to ovenware, fine china and ceramics as an art form. Lindroos's factory was considered a model for ceramic production at the time it was completed but is, like much of his work, quite undistinguished in architectural terms.

In Finland 1947 was not a rich year, architecturally speaking. Hugo Harmia and Woldemar Baeckman maintained their leading position within the profession by taking a joint second prize in the Tampere Technical High School competition. The other second-prize winner was Yrjö Lindegren of Helsinki Olympic Stadium fame.[48] A posthumous work by Uno Ullberg in partnership with Erkki Linnasalmi, the Helsinki Children's Clinic, should be mentioned as an important social contribution of this period.[49] Following the ravages and stresses of the war, such a children's facility was much needed in the capital at that time. There were also some private houses of interest, notably those at Nurmijärvi by Aarne Hytönen and Riisto-Veikko Luukonen and at Westend by Viljo Revell.[50]

In 1948 Aino and Alvar Aalto celebrated their twenty-fifth wedding anniversary. In the same year Alvar published his celebrated essay 'L'œuf de poisson et le saumon'[51] and prepared the design for the Strömberg Factory and Sauna at Vaasa.[52]

The results of the Salla Church competition (1948) once again showed that the winners, Eero Eerikäinen and Osmo Sipari, had been successful by following the direction set by Bryggman in his Turku Funeral Chapel.[53] What this competition really revealed, however, was a general tendency to move away from modernism towards this more romantic mode of expression. And indeed, the result of the Rovaniemi Church competition, which was announced at the same time, further confirmed the faltering of modernism in favour of such a compromise.[54]

From 1948 onwards there was also increasing contact between Finland and the United States. In that year, Ervi followed up the success of his Kestikartano Restaurant with a Finnish Restaurant at 39–41 East 50th Street in New York City.[55] *Arkkitehti* had previously only published the work of two contemporary American architects, Frank Lloyd Wright and, of course, Finnish-born Eliel Saarinen. In the autumn of 1948 the Association of Finnish Architects' journal reviewed two houses by Richard Neutra, one for Edgar Kaufmann at Palm Springs and another for a Mr Tremaine at Montecito, and in addition published some work by Walter Wurdeman and Paul Nelson.[56] Viljo Revell came into increasing prominence with the competition for a housing project in Vaasa,[57] while Erik Bryggman moved increasingly into the background when his design for the Turku University Library competition was unplaced in the winter of 1948.[58] Modernism, however, appeared to be set for a revival, at least at the hands of one of the younger generation of Finnish architects. Aulis Blomstedt's submission for the Turku University Library competition was certainly uncompromising in its functionalist expression.[59]

Unfortunately, one of the consequences of wars is the attention that must be given in their aftermath to the design of graveyards. Turku Cemetery (1929–35), the site of Bryggman's Turku Funeral Chapel, is acknowledged throughout the world as a masterpiece of Finnish graveyard design. It is a popular spot for relatives to this day and many continue the pagan and early Christian tradition by picnicking there during their visits on warm summer afternoons. In 1949 two outstanding graveyard designs were completed: one at Saynätsälo by Aulis Blomstedt and another at Hyvinkää by Erik Lindroos.[60]

Otherwise, the end of the decade is marked mainly by the construction of industrial and commercial work. Erkki Huttunen's mill and silos for SOK were completed during 1949,[61] as was his most memorable design, that for the SOKOS Building between Eliel Saarinen's Railway Station and Mannerheimintie in Helsinki.[62] The latter is

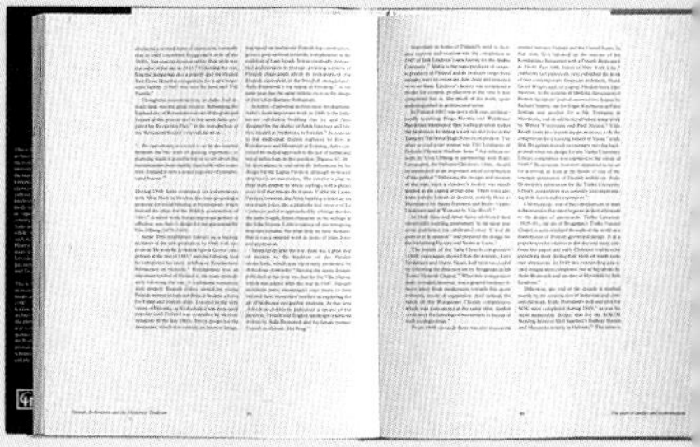

 Finnish Architecture in the Modernist Tradition.

Chapman & Hall | Malcolm Quantrill. London 1993.

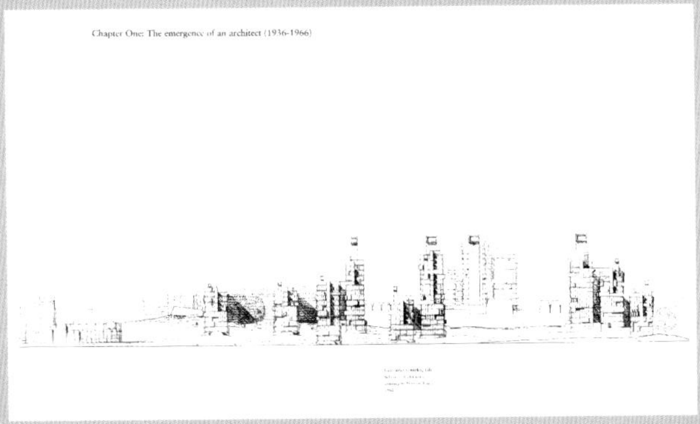

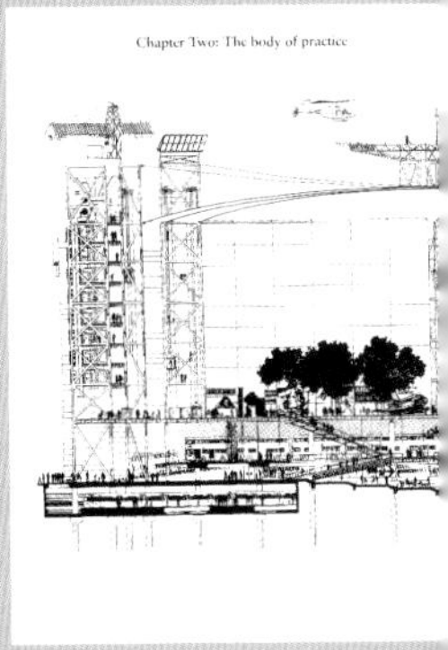

 The Norman Foster Studio.

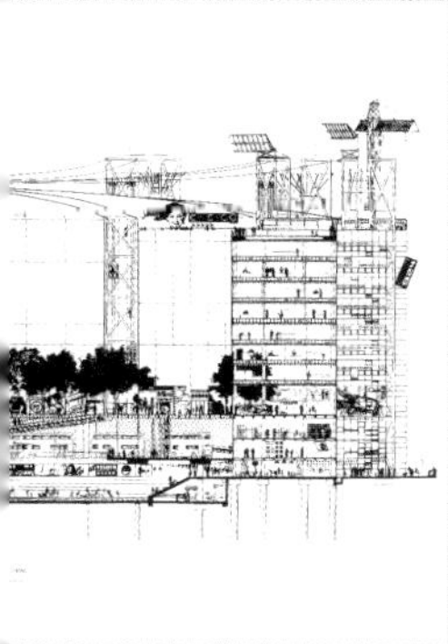

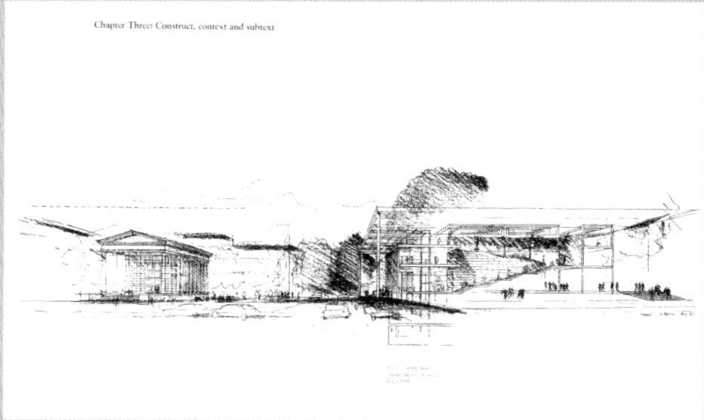
Chapter Three: Construct, context and subtext

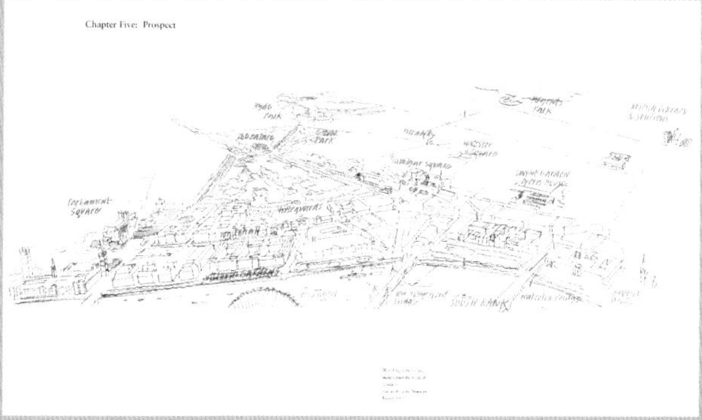
Chapter Five: Prospect

The Modern Steel House
Neil Jackson

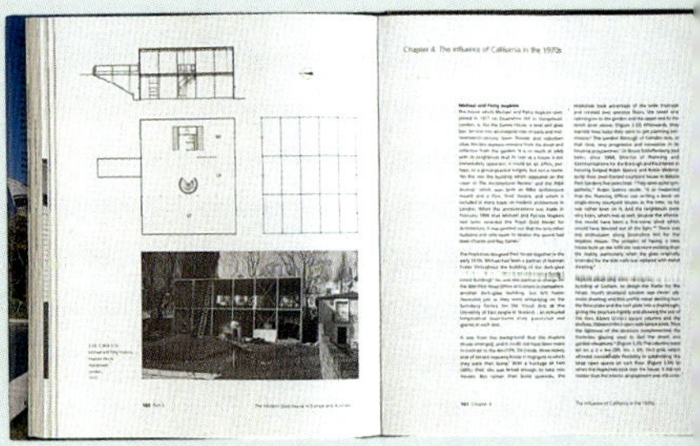

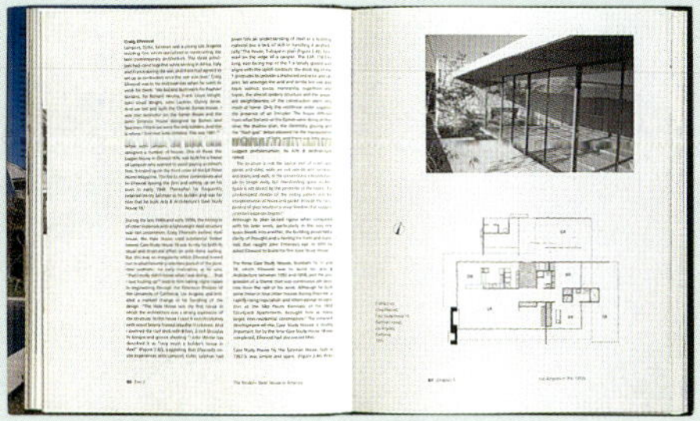

Chapman & Hall | Neil Jackson. London 1995.

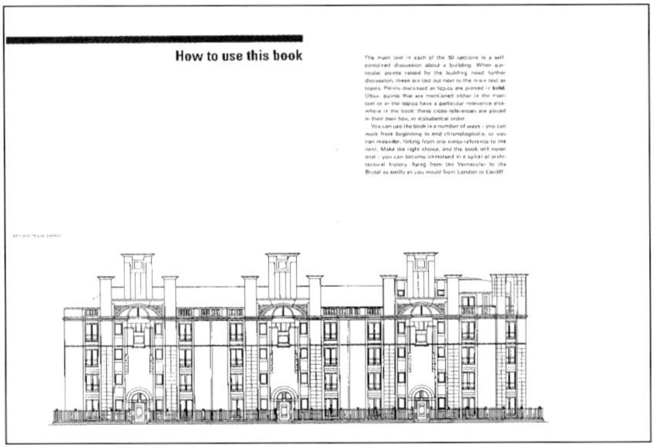

How to use this book

The main text in each of the 50 sections is a self-contained discussion about a building. When particular points raised by the building need further discussion, these are laid out next to the main text as topics. Points discussed as topics are printed in **bold**. Often, points that are mentioned either in the main text or in the topics have a particular relevance elsewhere in the book: these cross-references are placed in their own box, in alphabetical order.

You can use the book in a number of ways – you can work from beginning to end chronologically, or you can meander, flitting from one cross-reference to the next. Make the right choice, and the book will never end – you can become immersed in a spiral of architectural history, flying from the Vernacular to the Brutal as easily as you would from London to Cardiff.

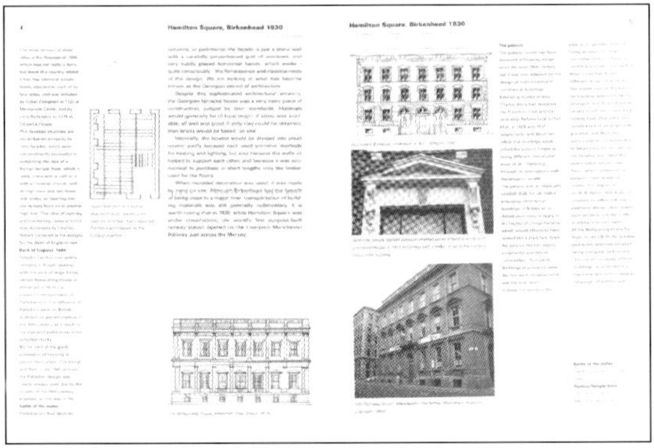

Hamilton Square, Birkenhead 1830

Hamilton Square, Birkenhead 1830

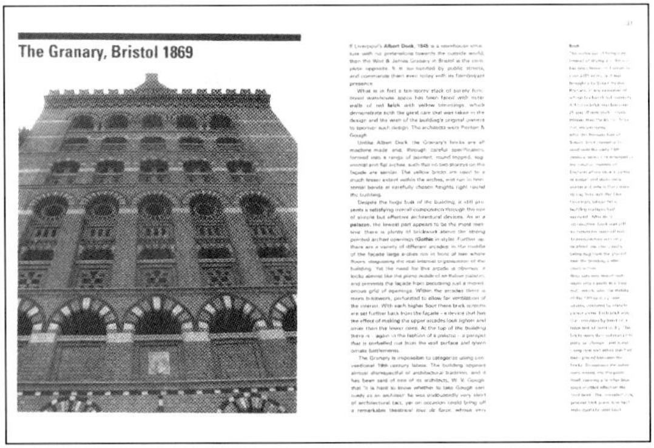

The Granary, Bristol 1869

If Liverpool's **Albert Dock, 1845** is a warehouse structure with no pretensions towards the outside world, then the Wait & James Granary in Bristol is the complete opposite. It is surrounded by public streets, and commands them even today with its flamboyant presence.

What is in fact a ten-storey stack of purely functional warehouse space has been faced with outer walls of red **brick** with yellow trimmings, which demonstrate both the great care that was taken in the design and the wish of the building's original owners to sponsor such design. The architects were Ponton & Gough.

onumental inscriptions fixed the shapes of the
alphabet. Informal written letters of the same date
ow their forms break down into minuscules, with
above and below the line. An A is made from
parate straight lines but if the pen is kept on the
e form changes to λ and when written quickly
ill or a laundry list scribbled on papyrus or wax in
century looks surprisingly like modern hand
even though the actual letterforms are
ar and almost illegible.
years passed before these changes were
ssed in serious writing. However, even in
e of the great formal scripts used for books
n the first and eighth centuries, some minuscule
begin to appear. The written letters nearest to the
onal capitals are called Quadrata or Square
. They retain a stately geometry and must have
w to write.
cs, a second formal book script, have slightly
sed letter forms, more suitable to calligraphy. The
oken by a few large letters, the u is inversed (a
per form) and the crossbar of the A disappears.
are less sombre and easier to read than Quadrata
they have no spaces between the words.
n Uncials, the book script used for many early
n documents, show some important changes in
elopment of lower case. The ascending and
ling strokes have become an important feature of
abet and, as a result, words can be recognized
sily.
0 700 many regional styles of book script were in
urope, as well as many informal hands. The Book
one of the most magnificent books ever produced
itten in the regional style current in the British Isles
as Anglo-Irish Half Uncials. The text is written in a
med minuscule alphabet, the ascenders and
ders properly form parts of letters and are no
accidental flourishes. The serifs are strong pen
apes, and not artificial constructions harking
capital letters.
e Capitals, Rustica and Uncials were still used
ings or for short lengths of text. By the end of the
entury the strength and legibility of the Anglo
ipt led Charlemagne to choose Alcuin of York to
se the new imperial scriptorium at Tours. A new
writing was needed to replace the current
styles in order to give the Emperor's documents
ional authority and clarity, just as a firm today
ve a house style designed to give its printed
nity and a clear identity.
ew script, known as Carolingian minuscules, was
ed at Tours and elsewhere in Europe from the
Irish Half Uncial and the local French book hand
as Merovingian. From it grew the great book

Settings of the text faces which appear in this atlas are shown overleaf. It is thus possible to compare the texture, colour, brilliance and legibility of each type when in use. However, to show the great variety of effects possible one would also need to compare the look of different leadings printed on different papers by several processes. The language itself might have an influence on the choice of face. Latin, for example, with its frequent c's, m's, n's and e's, looks quite different from English.

All but a few of our examples are in 10pt, variously leaded, and of equal column width. The ideal size, leading and 'measure' is, of course, dependent upon the use to which the type is put; each typeface requires careful individual consideration for its particular purpose. It would be also instructive to compare text settings of type of equal x-height.

Many new designs of text faces tend to be rather condensed, with short extenders, partly to save space. Type designers chop the extenders short to allow the lines to be crowded together; typographers space the lines out again to compensate for this mutilation. The result of this is often better and more legible than allowing the extenders to control the spaces between lines. Roman inscriptions and early printing produced fine textures, but we find them hard to read. Setting unleaded grotesques in text makes the page as even and orderly as a sheet of Zip-a-tone, and about as legible. But well-leaded grots have yet to be proved less legible than serifed faces. The length of a line and the relationship of point size to size of printed area are equally important considerations affecting legibility.

In letterpress printing, rough paper requires a heavy impression which thickens the letter forms, and smooth hard paper ever emphasizes the brilliance of types with strongly contrasting thick and thin strokes. This atlas is printed by offset-lithography which, owing to the thin ink used and the even contact of the offset roller with the paper, does not distort the image or thicken the forms, though the slight halation during the photographic preparation of the litho plate can cause a soft outline.

Improved techniques, however, especially on the Continent and in America, can give results as crisp and as black as letterpress. Lack of distortion and thickening allow modern text faces to be strongly drawn and very precise, though if the offset printer chosen is likely to give only average quality, a vigorous type of even weight is best, with open counters and, if serifed, well bracketed.

Photogravure gives half-tones the greatest delicacy and richness, but the fine screen, combined with the soft paper necessary to draw out the ink from the etched hollows in the gravure roller, tends to blur outlines, thicken strokes and break hairlines in lettering. Good results can only be obtained by restricting the choice of type to those having similar characteristics to those

e otomachia Poliphili. Aldus Manutius, Venice 1499

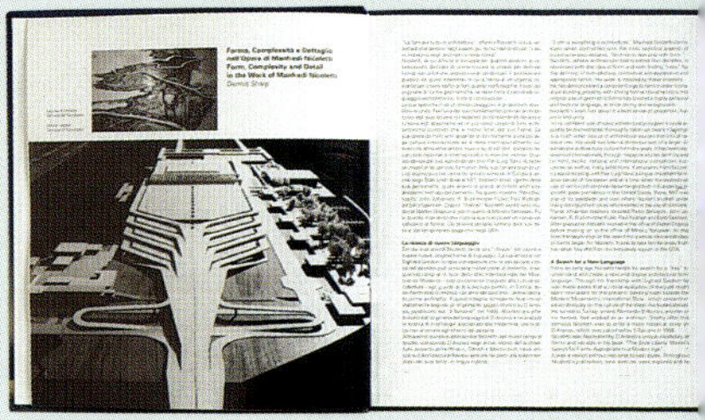

 Manfredi Nicoletti.

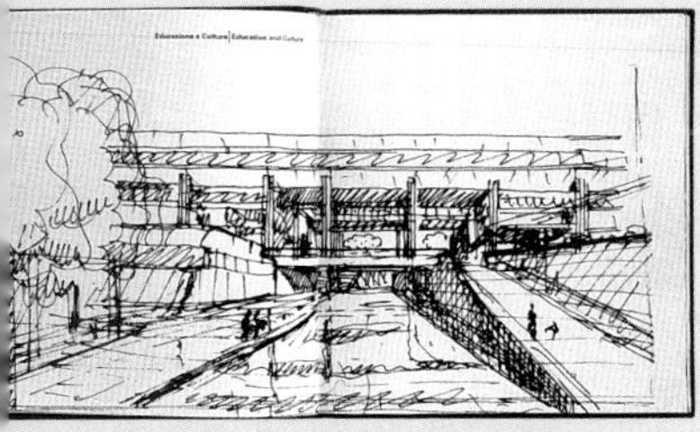
Educazione e Cultura | Education and Culture

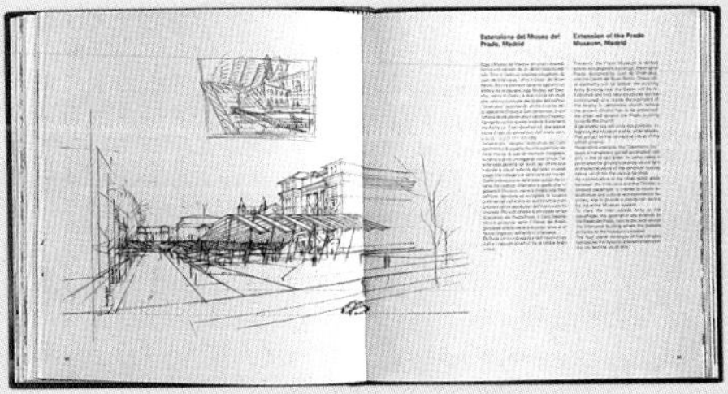
Estensione del Museo del Prado, Madrid
Extension of the Prado Museum, Madrid

The Idea of DOCOMOMO

Hubert-Jan Henket
Founding Chairman
DOCOMOMO International

This book presents a survey of buildings of a style and type that are not always popularly admired, largely because their unique origins are ill understood. Today, many of them are under serious threat of being lost to us through factors intimately related to those origins. But a growing international movement is working to reduce the misunderstandings and reverse this neglect. Why are these buildings so special and how has all this come about? Having stepped into the beginning of a new century let us step back to the early years of the last one.

In 1926 the young Dutch architect Jan Duiker was asked to design a sanatorium near Hilversum for the diamond workers of Amsterdam suffering from tuberculosis. He believed strongly in the rapidly developing areas of science and technology. His client, the Diamond Workers' Trade Union, shared with him the belief that effective medicines would be developed within twenty years there by rendering the sanatorium redundant. What purpose, therefore, would be served making a building having a longer technically viable existence than functionally required? True to the Modern Movement ideals of applying rational procedures for social ends, he designed a complex of buildings in which every space precisely fitted specific functions, employing a minimum use of materials and effort while exploiting technical innovation to the maximum. This approach he called 'spiritual economy' the result being both practically efficient and poetically beautiful. The quality of these buildings was such that many architects considered them among the most outstanding buildings of the twentieth century.

Following his death in 1934 Duiker's prescience was vindicated – by the early 1950s effective cures for tuberculosis had been evolved and the need for a sanatorium evaporated. This so called Zonnestraal complex was converted into a general hospital. For as long as the functional requirements remained unchanged Duiker's principle of 'spiritual economy' proved its worth, but when new uses were introduced the principle of tight fit between form and function became a liability. As a consequence, some elements of the complex were abandoned and fell into ruins while others were changed beyond recognition. Only the memories of a social and cultural monument survived. Gone were the poetry and beauty.

Even in the Netherlands Zonnestraal was not an isolated case. In that country alone there were many Modern Movement buildings of significant cultural value displaying similar social, technical and aesthetic characteristics whose fate and future usefulness were uncertain. Among these were such world-famous buildings as the van Nelle Factory by Van der Vlugt and the Kiefhoek housing estate by Oud, both in Rotterdam, and the Schröder House in Utrecht by Rietveld.

Faced with this new cultural phenomenon the Dutch Government Heritage Department approached me in 1982 to develop a methodology enabling them to make accountable decisions concerning culturally important Modern Movement buildings. Since Zonnestraal was notorious and technically the most complex, as well as being in dire need of intervention, it was used as the main research project for investigation. I invited a student of architecture who had special knowledge of Duiker's work, Wessel de Jonge, to assist in the project. One of the main recommendations in our final report was to contact architects and researchers faced with similar problems outside the Netherlands. To our great surprise colleagues in other countries were operating just like us in a similar ad hoc, isolated fashion notwithstanding the shared view that the Modern Movement has exerted the most significant influence on twentieth century architecture and urbanism.

Many questions emerged. Since it is not feasible to keep them all, which buildings and building groups should be conserved, and why? Each case is specific; not all buildings need the same type of protection. But what does protection imply? How is it possible to extend the economic and functional life of particular buildings in environmentally acceptable ways without sacrificing the authenticity of the original idea, including visual and tactile qualities? Can the paradox of preserving 'throw away' buildings be justified? In what way can experiences drawn from many countries be shared for mutual benefit? How can the public at large be informed of the cultural significance of the Modern Movement and those in power reminded of their responsibilities to celebrate and conserve our recent heritage?

These questions, and many more, convinced us of the need to get ourselves organised. In 1988 DOCOMOMO was founded at the School of Architecture in the Eindhoven University of Technology where I held a Chair in Building Technology. The memorable and rhythmic acronym DOCOMOMO was selected not only for its intrinsic appeal but, by placing

DOcumentation ahead of COnservation an inherent, realistic priority is established for posterity. In 1990 we organized the first international DOCOMOMO conference in Eindhoven. To our astonishment representatives from 13 countries arrived, all keen to join and launch Working Parties on their home territory. The question then arose, how to structure a voluntary organisation to unify disparate cultural, legal and hierarchical traditions. Wessel and I although interested in organizing DOCOMOMO for a few years were also busy as teachers and in practice and had no inclination to embed ourselves in bureaucracy. With the invaluable help of Christopher Dean, John Allan and James Dunnett from the United Kingdom we designed the DOCOMOMO constitution leaving each country to organise its own affairs within a unifying framework having minimum constraints. The rules would be formalised by a meeting of Council which consisted of representatives appointed by each National Working Party. One country, one vote. And so it happened! The constitution was accepted and DOCOMOMO was on its way.

Now, after twelve years, the network consists of active working parties in 40 countries and some 1400 participating architects, historians, students and technicians world wide. The International Secretariat once established in Eindhoven, was suddenly inundated by an avalanche of local initiatives from a diversity of locations such as La Plata in Argentina, Quebec in Canada and Belgrade in the former Yugoslavia, seeking help in the fight to protect their modern built heritage. Very often we had no idea of the importance of particular buildings or the urgency of the local situation. We were in danger of getting our priorities wrong

which would r
of the organiz
a register of t
each participa
the national d
by definition,
edge. In order
and oblige ea
a maximum o
allocated. The
and each con
our Modern M
donations hel
Movement as
variations and
representation
dubbed in 19
publication de

After a few ye
decided that
structured, an
with universal
documentatio
Committee fo
a standard fo
with a compre
The latter was
was invited by
Monuments a
proposal for M
(buildings and
World Heritag
set of criteria
buildings. In a
al registers, th
also asked to
prove sufficie
international
resulted so fa

6

...Otokuni, Kyoto 618-0071

...of 33 000m² near Kyoto, this is the ...ries of the experimental houses ...gated a type of Japanese dwelling ...signed to relate to the new modern ...d also Japanese climate. Scientific ...climate and the utilisation of ...raditional materials are the basis of ... The planning is totally controlled ... the design many new environmental ...as an underlaid ventilation system ...and the ceiling, the adoption of ...to protect from the strong sun ...cloud-wall to maintain the insulation.

4
Tokyo Detention Center
Kosuge, Katsushika, Tokyo 124-0001
1930
Shigeo Kanbara

This was built for the control office in the Tokyo Detention Center by Kanbara who was an architectural engineer of the ministry of Judicial Office. The front façade of the control office composed of the observation and clock tower, recalls a bird spreading its wings; it is one of the last examples in the movement of Expressionism in Japan since 1920s. He also designed in the Art Deco Style, the details of interior with his own aesthetic. Even though he adopted re-inforced concrete which was introduced in Japan at that time, he could manage to express dynamic form and sublime space, even in the restricted conditions associated within a detention center.

5
Tokyo Central Post Office
Marunouchi, Chiyoda-ku, Tokyo 100-0005
1931
Tetsuro Yoshida

A complex of two functions (central post and business office) is characteristic of modernism in the 1930s in Japan. Yoshida's Tokyo Central Post Office is a masterpiece and is sited in front of Tokyo Central Station. Although the planning of the building was started in 1922, the construction was not executed until 1927. ... earthquake and budgetary cutbacks, it was finally completed in 1931. Immediately, it was appreciated by Bruno Taut and also Japanese modernists as one of the best examples of new architecture in Japan. Yoshida was also famous for Deutsche-philia and published three books in German: 'Das Japanische Wohnhaus', 'Das Japanische Architektur', and 'Das Japanische Garten'.

6
Kameki Tsuchiura House
Kamiosaki, Shinagawa, Tokyo 141-0021
1935
Kameki Tsuchiura

This is representative of modern houses, which experimented with the adoption of the dry wall system. The influence from Walter Gropius is clearly seen in the building. Kameki Tsuchiura who was the owner and also the designer of the building, and worked for Frank Lloyd Wright at Taliesin. Nobu Tsuchiura, his wife, was also an architect and studied under Wright. With his encounter with Czech architect, B Feuerstein who worked for Perret, Tsuchiura developed his design ideas that he started with Wright's style, that later included Perret's, and finally he then arrived at the International Style. He designed 26 modern houses from 1931 to 1939 when he moved to Manchuria.

7
Keio Gijyuku Grade School
Ebisu, Shibuya, Tokyo 150-0013
1937
Yoshiro Taniguchi

There were only few architects who considered environmental planning in design practice in the 1930s. Taniguchi was one of them when he designed this grade school based on the theme of function and hygiene. He proposed new environmental engineering, such as ... a glass curtain wall to enrich openness, planting grass on the terrace to ease reflecting sunshine, and using a panel heating system. He challenged and created several new concepts, such as the interior facilities when he designed clover-typed desks for the workshop in the science classroom. This school is one of the best examples of a modern school in the pre-war Japan.

8
Ube City Public Hall
Asahi, Ube, Yamaguchi 755-0041
1937
Togo Murano

The building is dedicated to Yusaku Watanabe and six companies, who developed Ube city from a rural town to an industrial city. Thus the Ube City Public Hall is also a memorial hall and cultural center, in this region, and symbolizes modern industrial utopia. Its symmetrical composition creates a very strong impression with its simple volumetric shapes, curving brick covered front facade, and six tall concrete pylons in front of the entrance plaza. The symmetrical fan-shaped form, rightly follows the three functions which are a stage, an auditorium and an entrance hall. In particular, the entrance hall and second floor foyer have equally curved spaces in which their simplicity is underscored by their cylindrical columns.

9
Mayumi-no-ma, Hasshokan
Hiroji, Showa-ku, Nagoya 466-0834
1950
Sutemi Horiguchi

This was built as accommodation for the Emperor Showa, when he attended the Aichi National Athletic Games. Horiguchi understood that modern architecture was composed of lines and planes as its aesthetic principle ... He also insisted that the Japanese tradition was also composed of such aesthetics. He had a particular theory, that the Japanese tea ceremony room expresses an aesthetic work with in one space, and that the aesthetic composition of pillar, shoji, and tatami mats, are the essence of Japanese architecture. This accommodation space, was designed under Horiguchi's principle of aesthetic composition, which was to apply the motif of traditional architecture, such as that by Katsura Villa.

10
Kamakura Modern Art Museum
Kanagawa Prefecture
Yukinoshita, Kamakura, Kanga...
1951
Junzo Sakakura

The Museum was built beside ... pond which is located in the p... Kamakura Hachimangu Shrine ... the Kamakura era (1192-1333) ... Sakakura, who was the ... under Le Corbusier from 1931 ... returned to Japan because he ... grande prix for designing the J... ...ion for the Paris Exposition in ... of the architects who contribute... influences to the Japanese arc... both before and after the war. ... encloses a central courtyard. ... first floor, is divided by a maso... stone, and a slender steel fram... the exhibition space on the se...

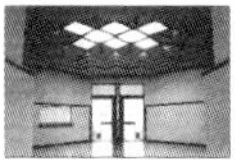

This bibliography combines key texts of the Modern Movement with a selection of later histories and commentaries. Monographs on individual architects are so numerous that these are only included for a few architects whose work was seminal to the development of the whole international movement. For extensive bibliographies on individual architects readers are referred to: Sharp D, **Sources of Modern Architecture: A critical bibliography** (London 1981) in the list of books below. Likewise works on individual countries are only included where these are under-represented in the general literature.

Catherine Cooke | Dennis Sharp

Books

Arkin D (ed)
Arkhitektura sovremennog...
Moscow 1932

Banham R
Theory and Design in th...
Machine Age
London 1960

Banham R
Guide to Modern Archite...
London 1962
New edition as:
Age of the Masters
London & New York 1975

Banham R
The New Brutalism
Stuttgart, London & New Y...

Banham R
The Architecture of the W...
tempered Environment
London & Chicago 1969

Bargellini P & Freyrie E
Nascita e vita dell' archit...
moderna
Florence 1947

Bauer C
Modern Housing
New York 1934

Baužienė M (ed)
Lietuvos Moderno Pastat...
Vilnius 1998

Bayer H, Gropius W & Gr...
Bauhaus 1919-1928
New York 1938, London 19...
German edition Stuttgart 1...

Behrendt C
Modern Building
London 1938

274

le being equally and thoroughly docu-
probably one of the most extensive
of documentation in the history of
ure. Over three hundred DOCOMOMO
s from across the world participated in
operation under the guidance of
ve chairs of the International
l Committee: Gerard Monnier from
ance; France Vanlaethem from
Canada; Maristella Casciato from
aly. Other major contributions have
m Marieke Kuipers (The
nds), Allen Cunningham (UK) and
nlham (Scotland). This book can only
a small number of buildings from the
rnational DOCOMOMO selection on
tailed information fiches have been
. The complete archive is held at the
ds Architectuurinstituut (NAi) in
n and is available for study.
, the DOCOMOMO working parties are
g the documentation of significant
Movement urban sites and land
which will be ready in 2004.

antime, what happened to
aal? A lot, and yet nothing. Many
nitiatives emerged. These included a
e resort for trade union members, an
re, a meditation resort, and a preven-
curative centre for heart patients; all
were investigated. The general
has departed, the buildings are empty,
storation or conversion work has
ue to lack of money, bureaucracy,
g interests, demanding requirements
ed expectations. Zonnestraal provides
of of the necessity for such buildings to
ered with, and kept under the continu-
ance of an organization like DOCOMO-

MO. We receive many complaints from all over the world about the general lack of interest in preservation of twentieth century architecture and urbanism. I even experience this incredible lack of understanding and care in the highest echelons of international heritage circles. Not only buildings like Duiker's Zonnestraal, Aalto's Viipuri library, Ginzburg's Narkomfin housing in Moscow but also, many lesser known masterpieces around the world were designed to fit the demands of our dynamic era. Precisely because of that they are easy prey to rapid change or demolition – often before it is recognized they are under threat.

And yet their social, technical and aesthetic innovations are representative of the best architecture of our time, and for many of us these are objects which, quite simply, we love. This book shows clearly the rich variety and exceptional architectural quality of Modern Movement buildings. They belong to the continuity of our civilisation and varied cultures and must be retained in one form or another for the enjoyment of future generations. This is a responsibility for us all.

Postscript
Literally on the day this book is being sent to the printers, good news for Zonnestraal has finally emerged after some 18 years of continuous struggle. All parties concerned have signed a covenant agreeing the future use of the complex, the restoration work to be done, the degrees of intervention to be allowed, the time-table and above all the financing. This optimistic future for Zonnestraal is in line with the optimistic ideas and endeavours characterizing the Modern Movement, hard to realize but very much worthwhile.

7

10
Agricultural Bank of Iceland
Austurstræti 5, 101 Reykjavik
1945 | 1948
Gunnlaugur Halldorsson

In the Agricultural Bank in Reykjavik, Halldorsson used a concrete column structure to create a free plan and a non-load-bearing glass façade. The site was very narrow and deep, connecting two parallel streets across a city block. This enabled the architect to develop a new and democratic concept for a modern banking hall which was bright and open and encouraged the man in the street to pass through. The building was a modern design in every detail, such as furnishings and lighting fixtures. Original furnishings in the banking hall were designed by Skarphedinn Johannsson and chairs in the director's office were by the Danish designer Børge Mogensen.

Progressive Icelandic artists of the time, painter Jon Engilberts and sculptor Sigurjon Olafsson, were brought in by the architect to do wall paintings and decorations. The elevation towards Austurstræti is still intact and important parts of the banking hall interior have survived.

Selected Bibliography :

Hannesson G
Um skipulag bæja. Arbok Haskola Islands
Reykjavik 1916

Agustsson H
Gunnlaugur Halldorsson arkitekt: foreword to exhibition catalogue
Reykjavik 1989

Armannsson PH
Einar Sveinsson arkitekt og husameistari Reykjavikur
Reykjavik 1995

Wedebrunn O (ed)
Modern Movement Scandinavia
Copenhagen 1998

Illustrations courtesy DOCOMOMO Iceland

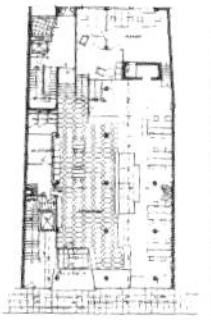

144

Cetto ML
Modern Architecture in Mexico
Stuttgart & London 1961

Cheney S
The New World Architecture
London 1930

CIAM (eds)
Die Wohnung für das Existenzminimum: Auf Grund der Ergebnisse des II Internationalen Kongresses für Neues Bauen
Frankfurt am Main 1930, repub Stuttgart 1933

CIAM (eds)
Rationelle Bebauungsweisen. Ergebnisse des 3 Internationalen Kongresses für Neues Bauen
Stuttgart 1931

Cohen J-L & Eleb M
Casablanca: Mythes et figures d'une aventure urbaine
Paris 1998

Collins P
Changing Ideals in Modern Architecture
London 1965

Cunningham A (ed)
Modern Movement Heritage
London 1998

Curtis WJR
Modern Architecture since 1900
London 1982 and later editions

Czerner O & Listowski H
Awangarda Polska. Architektura i Urbanistyka 1918-1939
Warsaw & Paris 1981

Deutscher Werkbund
Bau und Wohnung. Die Bauten der Weissenhofsiedlung in Stuttgart errichtet 1927; 'Die Wohnung'
Stuttgart 1927

Doesburg T van
De Stijl en de Europese architectuur
Nijmegen 1986
German translation as
Über Europäische Architektur
Basel 1990
English translation as
On European Architecture: complete essays from 'Het Bouwbedrijf' 1924-1931
Basel 1990

Dorfles G
L'architettura moderna
Milan 1954

Ferriss H et al
Machine Age Exposition catalogue
New York 1927

Frampton K
Modern Architecture. A Critical History
London 1980
French translation as
Histoire critique de l'architecture moderne
Paris 1985

Fry EM & Drew J
Tropical Architecture in the Dry and Humid Zones
New York 1964

Giedion S
Space, Time and Architecture
Cambridge (Mass) 1941 repub 1982

Giedion S
A Decade of New Architecture
Zürich & New York 1951

Ginzburg M
Zhilishche
Moscow 1934

Gossel P & Leuthauser G
Architecture in the 20th Century
Cologne 1990

Gropius W
Internationale Architektur
Munich 1925 repub 1927

Gropius W
The New Architecture and the Bauhaus
London 1936
German edition 1965

Herbert G
Martienssen and the International Style
Cape Town 1975

Heynen H
Architecture and Modernity: A Critique
Cambridge (Mass) 1999

Hitchcock H-R
In the Nature of Materials: the buildings of Frank Lloyd Wright 1887-1941
New York 1942, repub London 1973

Hitchcock H-R & Johnson P
The International Style. Architecture since 1922
New York 1932 repub 1966

Hitchcock H-R
Latin American Architecture since 1945
New York 1955

Jackson N
The Modern Steel House
London 1996

Jencks C
Modern Movements in Architecture
Harmondsworth 1973

Joedicke J
A History of Modern Architecture
Stuttgart & London 1959

Joedicke J
Architecture since 1945
Stuttgart & London 1972

Joedicke J & Plath C
Die Weissenhofsiedlung Stuttgart
Stuttgart 1977

Johansson G
Funktionalismen i Verkligheten
Stockholm 1931

Johnson P & Hitchcock H-R et al
Modern Architecture International Exhibition: catalogue
New York 1932

Johnson P
Mies van der Rohe
New York 1947

Jong C & Mattie E
Architectural Competitions: vol I 1792-1949, vol II 1950-Today
Cologne & Naarden 1994

Kirsch K
Werkbund ausstellung 'Die Wohnung' Stuttgart 1927. Die Weissenhofsiedlung
Stuttgart 1993

Klotz H (ed)
Vision der Moderne. Das Prinzip Konstruktion
Munich 1986

Kopp A
Quand le moderne n'était pas un style mais une cause
Paris 1988

Krischanitz A & Kapfinger O
Die Wiener Werkbundsiedlung. Dokumentation einer Erneuerung
Vienna 1985

Lampugnani VM (ed)
Encyclopaedia of 20th Century Architecture
London 1986

Lange E de
Geen Officiële maar Levende Schoonheid: het internationale nieuwe bouwen tot 1940
's Gravenhage 1983

Le Corbusier
Vers une architecture
Paris 1923
English translation as
Towards a New Architecture
London 1929

Le Corbusier
Urbanisme
Paris 1925
English translation as
The City of Tomorrow and its Planning London 1929
Russian translation with additions as **Planirovka goroda**
Moscow 1933

Le Corbusier
The Athens Charter
New York 1973

Lesnikowski W (ed)
East European Modernism: Architecture in Czechoslovakia Hungary & Poland between the Wars
London & New York 1996

Lindner W & Steinmetz G
Die Ingenieurbauten und ihre Entwicklung
Leipzig 1923

Loghem JB van
Bouwen. Bauen. Bâtir. Building.
Amsterdam 1932 repub Nijmegen 1980

Lopez Rangel R
La Modernidad aquitectonica mexicana 1900-1940
Azcapotzalco 1989

Lundahl G (ed)
Nordisk Funktionalisme
Uppland 1980

Machedon L & Scoffham E
Romanian Modernism: The Architecture of Bucharest 1920-1940
Cambridge (Mass) 1999

Mambriani A
L'Architettura Moderna nei paesi Balcani
Bologna 1970

Meyer P
Moderne Architektur
Zürich 1928

Minorski J
Polska Mysl Innowacyjna w Architekturze 1918-1939
Warsaw 1970

Moholy-Nagy L
Von Material zu Architektur
Munich 1929
English translation as
The New Vision from Material to Architecture
New York 1930

Monnier G
L'architecture du XXe siècle
Paris 1997

Moravanszky A
Die Erneuerung der Baukunst. Wege zur Moderne in Mitteleuropa 1900-1940
Salzburg 1988

Müller M
Architektur und Avantgarde
Frankfurt am Main 1984

Myers IE
Mexico's Modern Architecture
New York 1952

Newman O
CIAM '59 in Otterlo: themes buildings, projects
London 1961

275

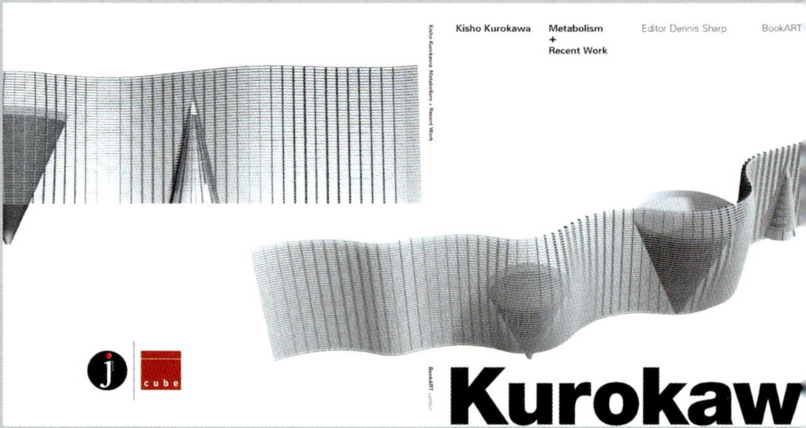

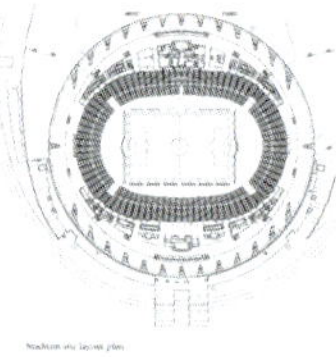

Stadium site layout plan

Known as 'Big Eye' the Oita Stadium is one of the chosen venues for the next World Cup in 2002. It will be reused for the second stage of the Japan Inter-Prefectural Athletic Competition in 2008 after the World Cup continuing to grow in the future to become a large scale all-purpose sports park for Oita.

The whole site covers an area of 255 ha. and has several facilities outside the main football stadium. These include general fitness, training and lodging centres, a botanical pool, two multi-purpose athletic fields, two rugby and soccer practice pitches, a softball field, tennis courts and other games areas.

The main stadium features an open track for athletic events as well as the football pitch. It can also be used year-round for public events aided by its retractable roof. For soccer matches, spectator seats are placed right up to the edge of the pitch to bring them close to the action. To change over for track events a retractable seating system was developed.

The stadium sits elegantly on its site, enhanced by the gentle curves of its spherical design. The choice of the sphere, Kurokawa says, is 'an expression of abstract symbolism'. This spherical shape also enables the retractable portion to move along its curved surface. The use of Teflon membrane panels with 25% light permeability obviates the need for artificial lighting during daylight hours. In order for the pitch to get proper exposure to sunlight the elliptical roof opening runs along the north-south axis. A main arch with perpendicular horizontal sub members follows the elliptical shape of the roof opening. As a type of large space frame this 'pipe-arch' structure is economical. Between the roof and the spectator seating below the surrounding mountains can be seen from a slender ventilation clearstorey set just below the roof line. This slit of space is designed to create a feeling of openness inside the stadium. Since the original design, an idea emerged for a moving camera to be located on the main beam to deliver special dynamic images for television audiences around the world.

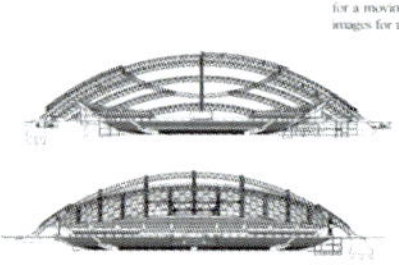

Cross section (above) and longitudinal section

38

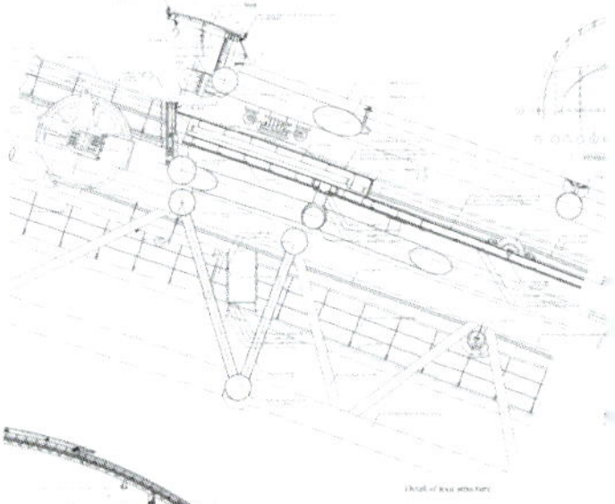

Detail of roof structure

Detailed section through roof stand and roof

Kisho Kurokawa

Metabolism
+
Recent Work

Guangzhou Pearl Riverside Area | China 2001

Component Design

 Rip-off Ray & Charles Eames. London 1997.

SMOOTHNESS.
THE MEN OF
AND
HAD IT.
TEACHERS

 Mahesh Patel. Rain perfume. London 1997.

70 TEC shopfront with Craig Downie. London 1996.

NEXT
125
NEXT TEP
TELEPHONE 081 896
CAREERS
TRAINING

 Fast-food concession with Graínne Egan. London 1984.

Continental Insurance. London 1985.

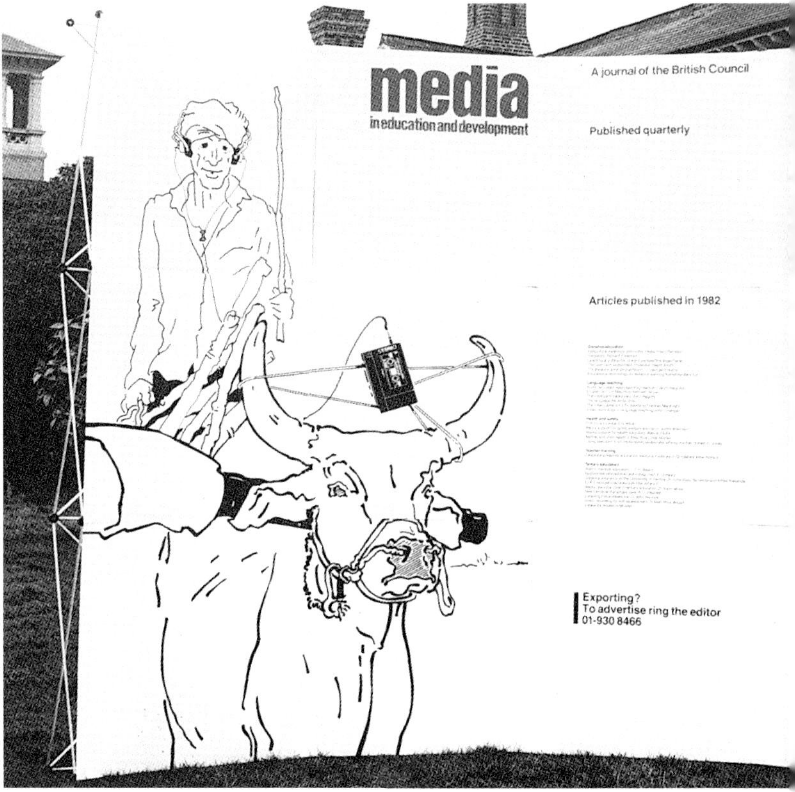

The British Council. London 1982.

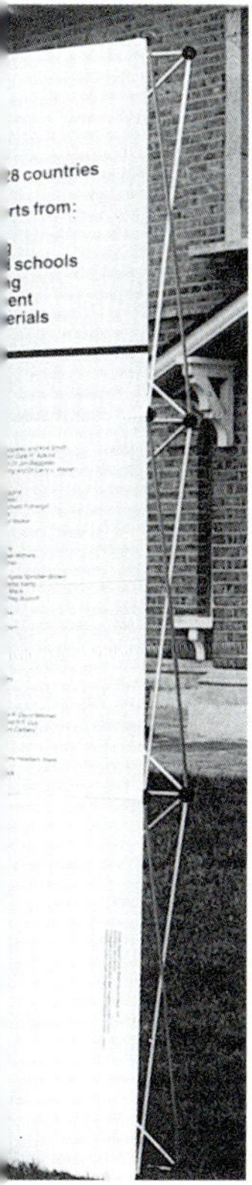

Video covers. The Building Centre Trust. London 1998.

76 Eastern Arts Lottery bid. London 1992.

Kisho Kurokawa. London 1998.

 Easter gifts. London 1992.

 Thames TV promotion. London 1969.

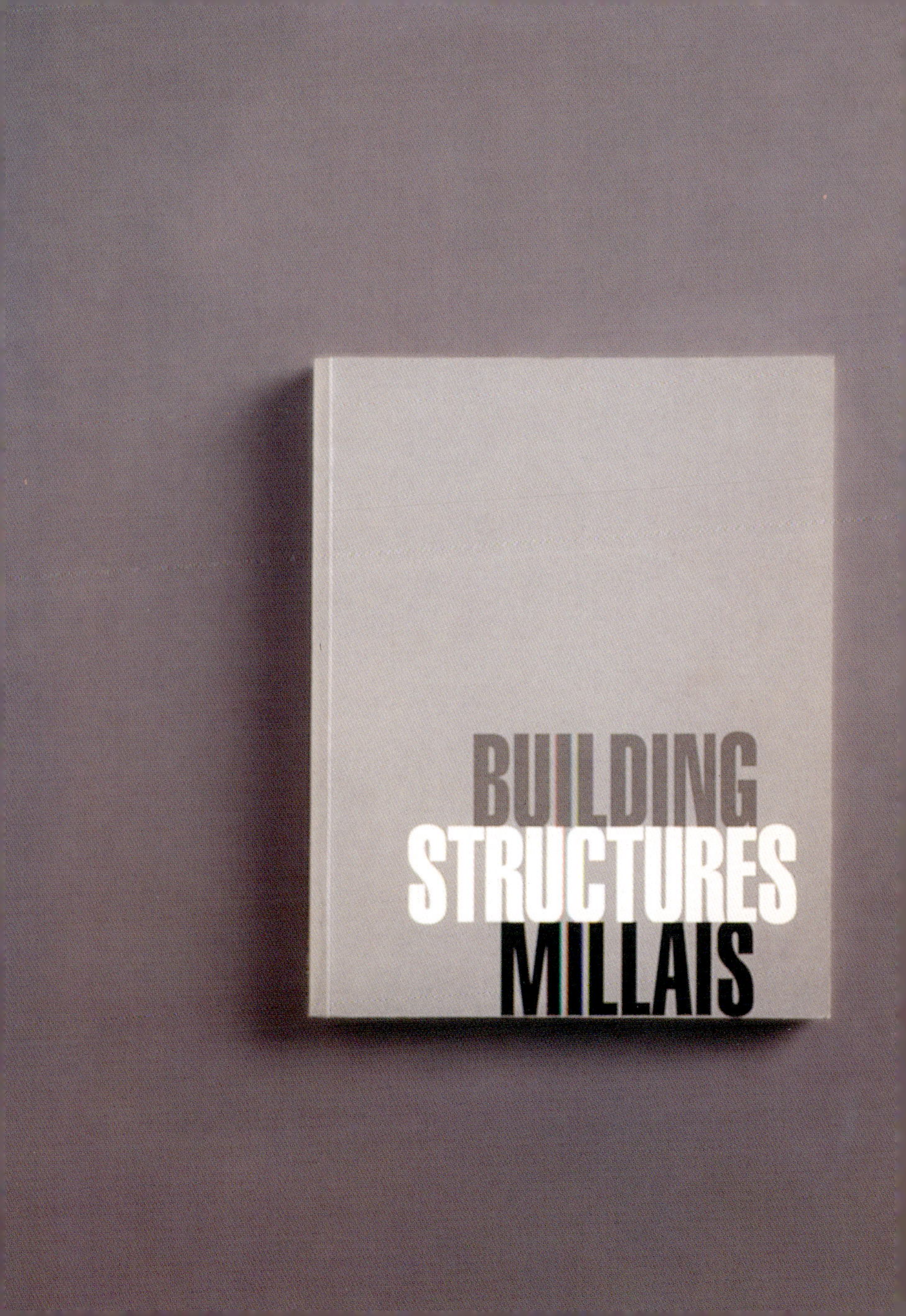
BUILDING
STRUCTURES
MILLAIS

STRUCTURAL GLASS
Peter Rice and Hugh Dutton
Structural Glass
Second edition

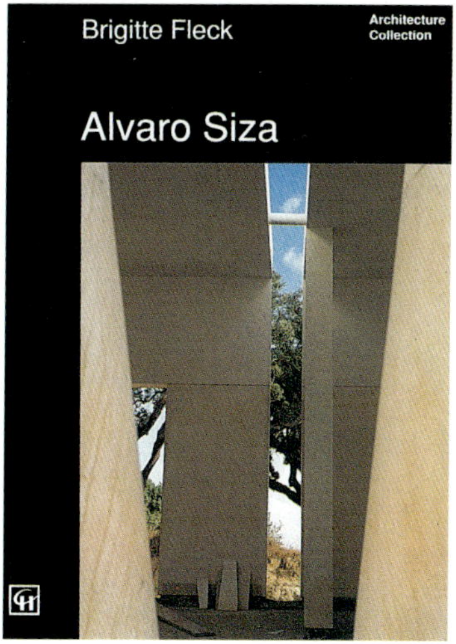

Chapman & Hall. London 1994.

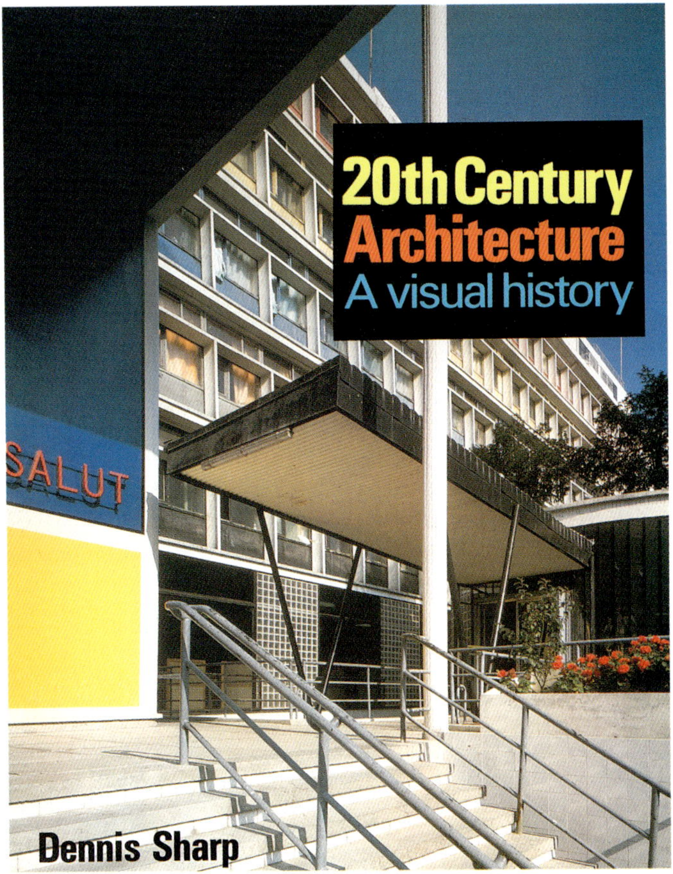

 Lund Humphries. London 1995.

The British Council. London 1982.

BookArt. London 1994. Second edition 1997.

 Chapman & Hall. London 1994.

Santiago Calatrava
editor Dennis Sharp

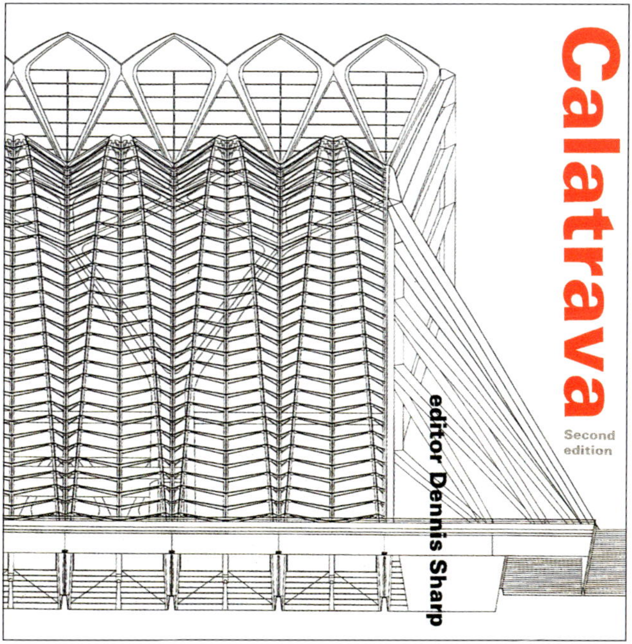
Calatrava
Second edition
editor Dennis Sharp

 Phaidon Press. London 1992.

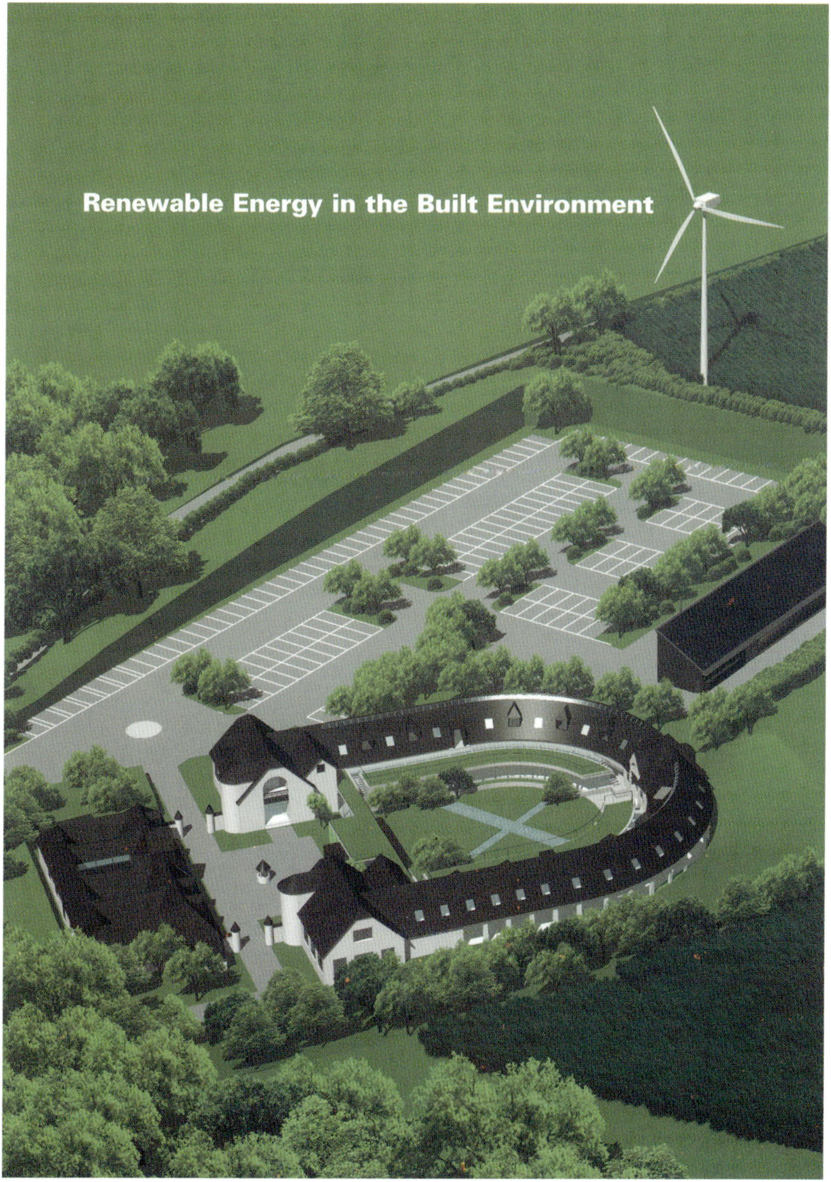

The Building Centre Trust. London 2002.

The
Thom Gorst
Buildings
Around
Us

The Modern Statio
New approaches to railway architect
Brian Edwa

Chapman & Hall. London 1993.

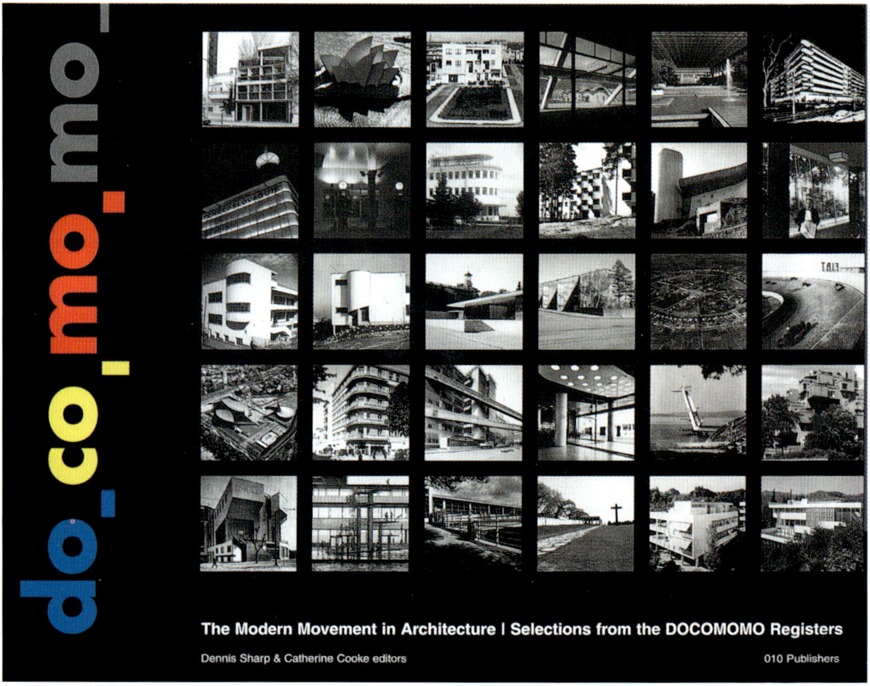

 010 Publishers Rotterdam. London 2000.

The Images Publishing Group, *Yearbook 8,* first visual concept. London 2001.

ROSSELLI
Paolo Rosselli | Anthony Tischhauser

with

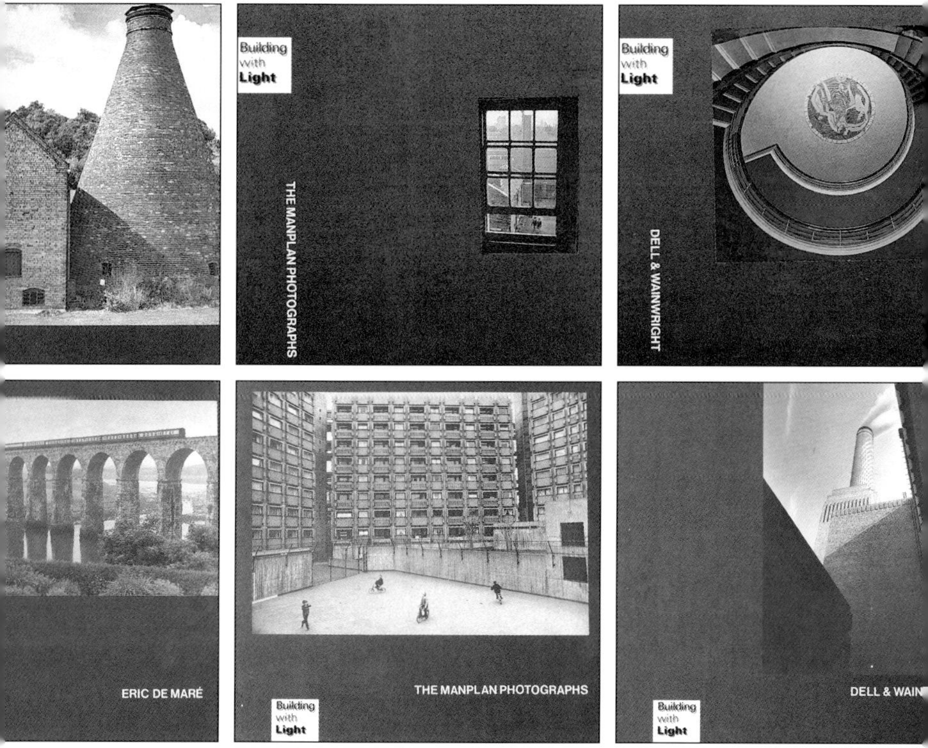

Alternative covers. Architectural photography series. London 1997.

Norman and British Romanesque

A comparative architectural study of Naves Choirs and Transepts

Paul Drake

96 Paul Drake. London 1998.

RIBA|AIJ|1996
新進気鋭の
日本の建築家たち
EXHIBITION 25.3 – 16.4

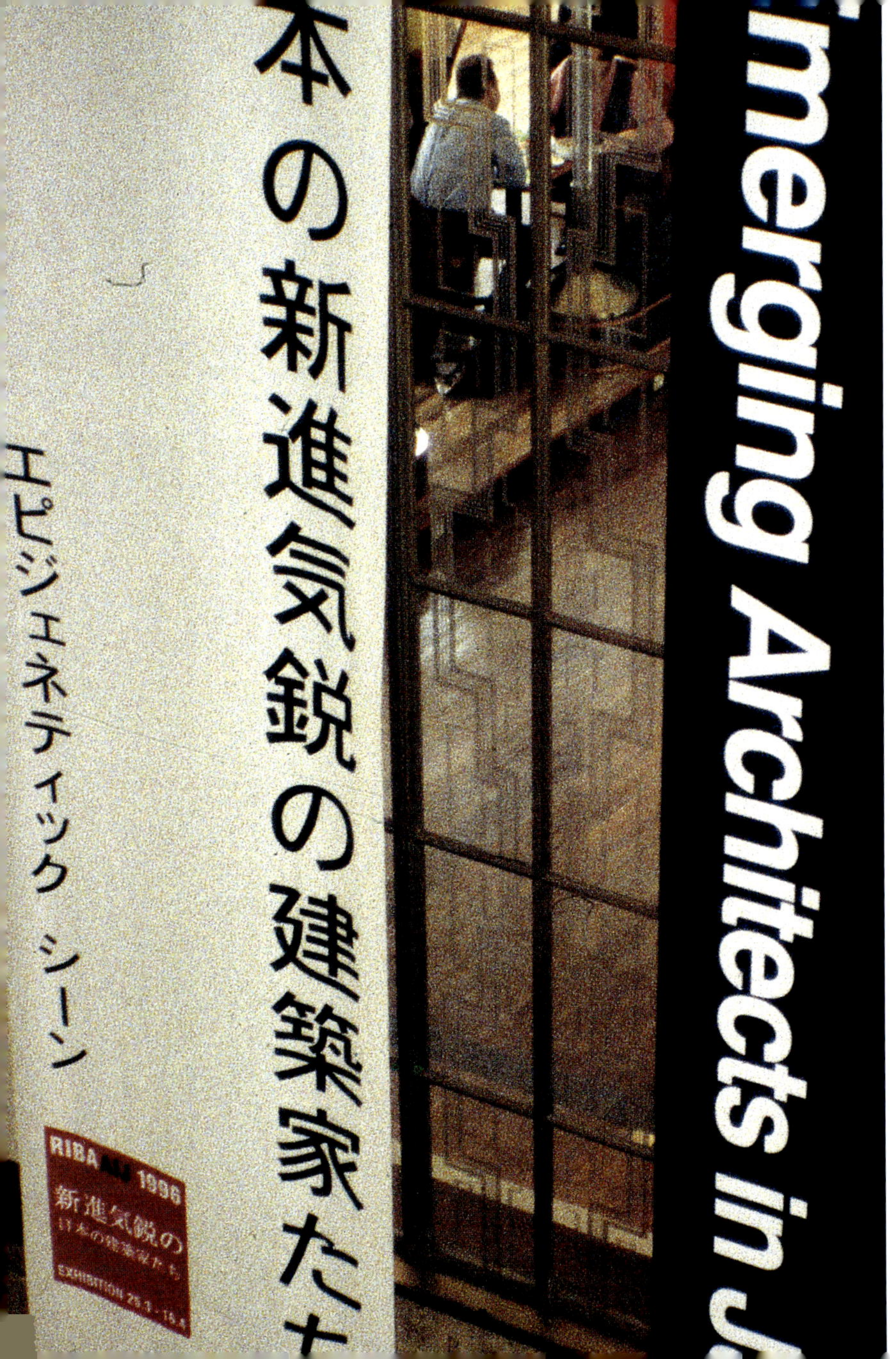
本の新進気鋭の建築家た
エピジェネティック シーン
RIBA
1996
新進気鋭の
merging Architects in

Emerging Japanese Architects exhibition. Folding mailed poster. London 1997.

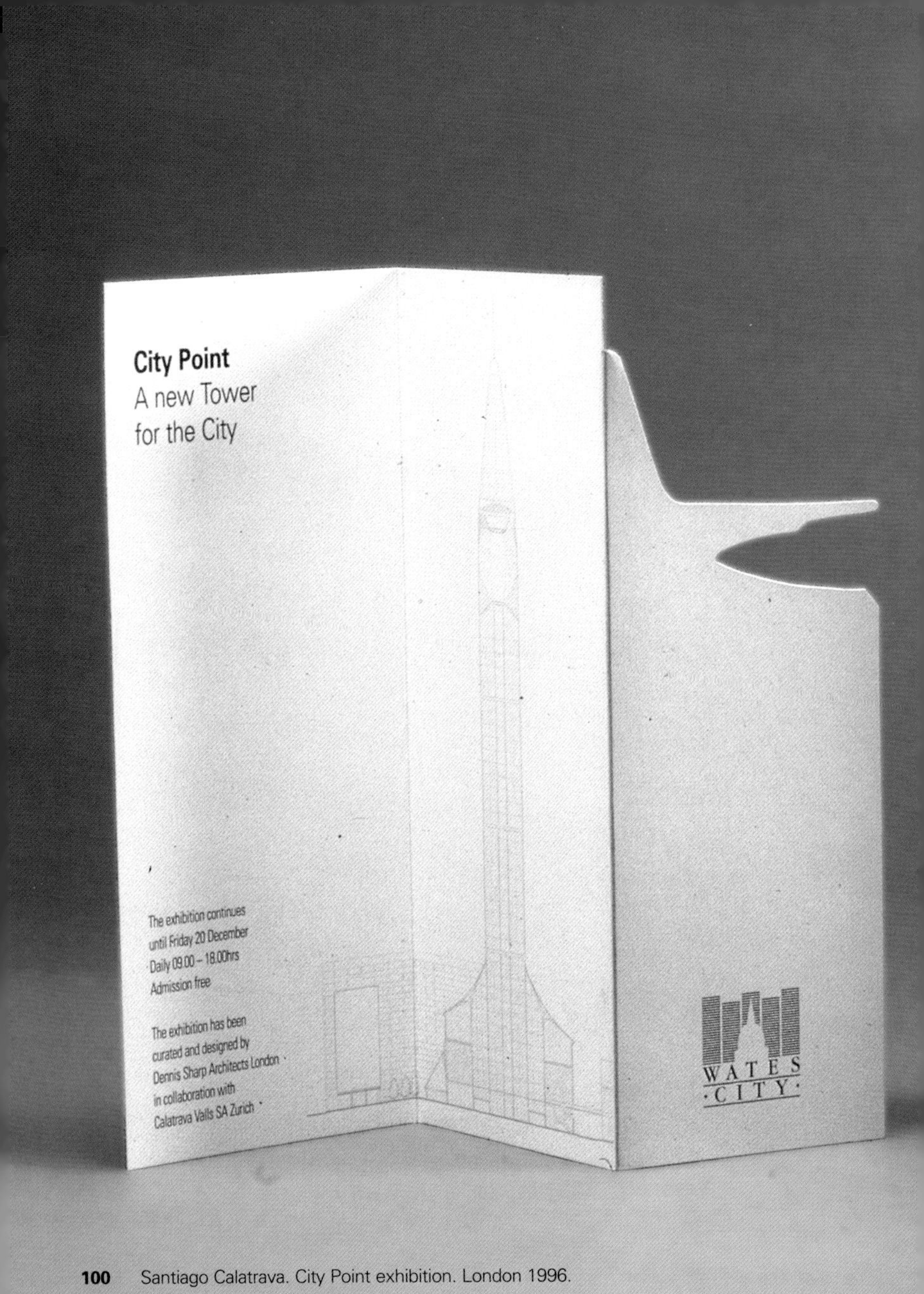

100 Santiago Calatrava. City Point exhibition. London 1996.

City Point exhibition
private view
Exhibition of
design proposals for Britannic
Tower by Santiago Calatrava
Wednesday 27 November 1996
18.30hrs
Britannic Tower
Ground floor gallery
Ropemaker Street, London EC2
And later at 20.00hrs, in
the theatre auditorium, an illustrated
lecture by Santiago Calatrava
discussing his proposals
Drinks and canapes
RSVP Please use enclosed card

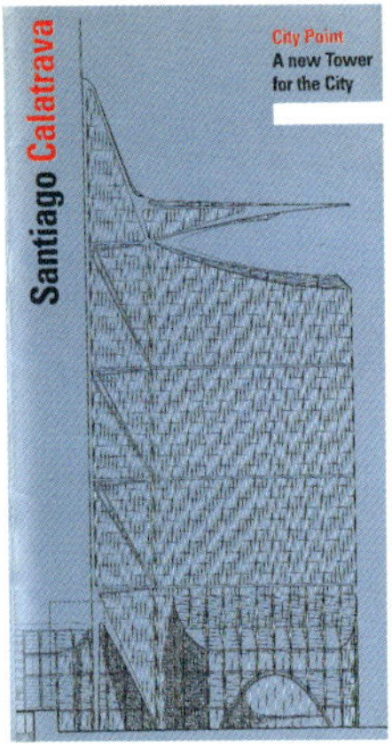
Santiago Calatrava
City Point
A new Tower for the City

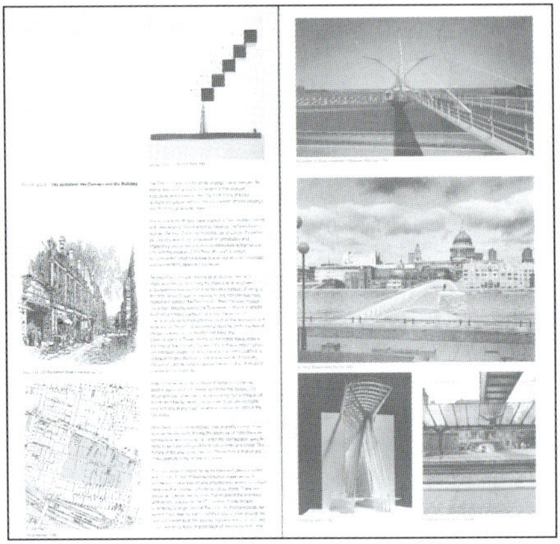

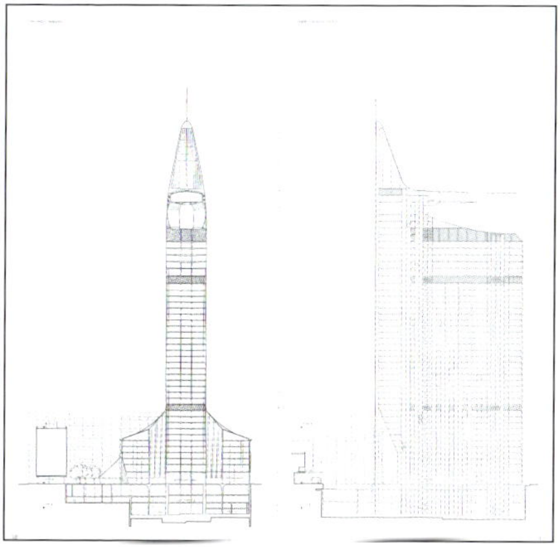

Santiago Calatrava. City Point. London 1996.

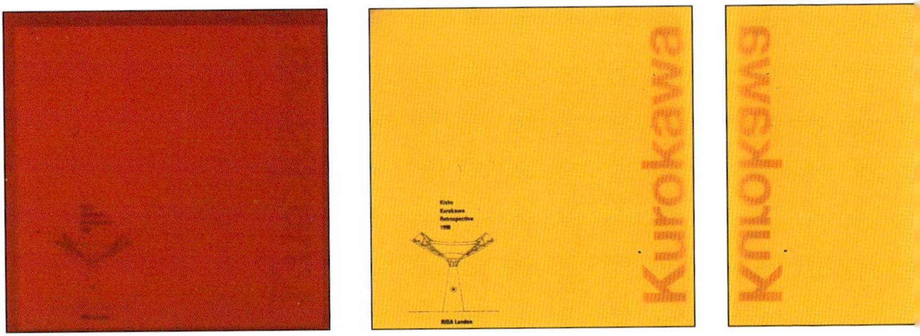

 Kisho Kurokawa exhibition. London 1998.

Kurokawa

You are cordially invited to the opening

Kisho Kurokawa Retrospective
'From the Age of the Machine to the Ag

Thursday 16 April 1998 6.30pm at the
RIBA Architecture Centre
66 Portland Place London W1N 4AD

RSVP: Acceptances telephone 0171 30

please bring this card with you to the opening

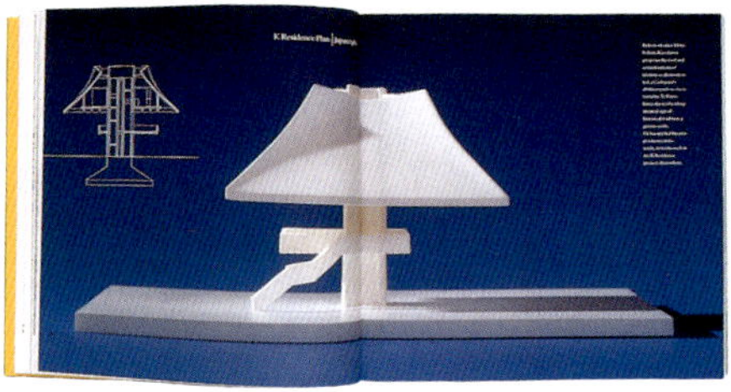

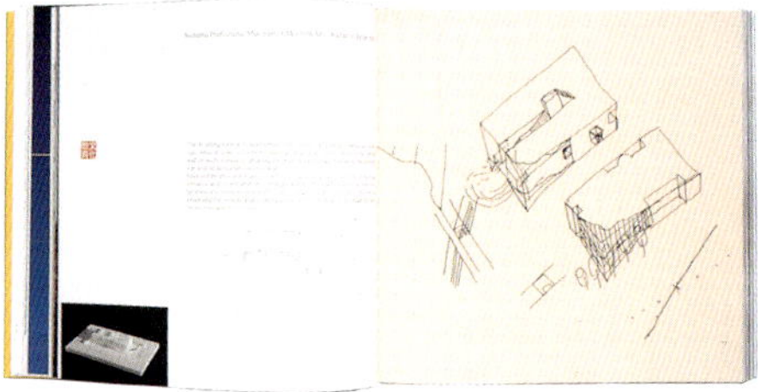

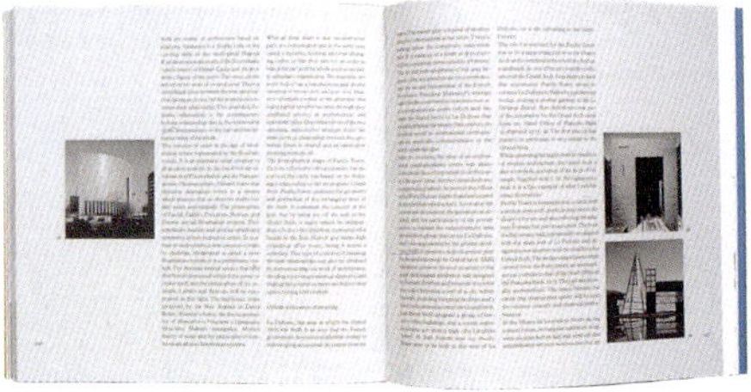

 Kisho Kurokawa. London 1998.

Exhibition invitation with Bob Clift. London 2001.

108 Connell Ward & Lucas exhibition. London 1994.

Connell Ward & Lucas

Modern Movement Architects in England 1929–1939

Editor Dennis Sharp

BOOK ART | LONDON

House
Wentworth, Surrey

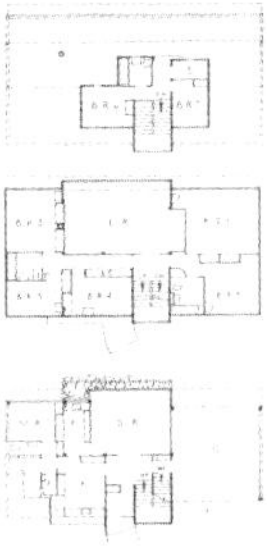

Connell's African Years

Connell, Ward and
be complete without
Connell's post-war
in East Africa. In the
ive climate he found
able to reconcile his
fluences, his rational
his innovative ideas for
l version of modern
One or two of these
eve high standards
cessful innovative
those at Grayswood
ead although far more
anything he or his
ied out in Britain in
work heralded the
a new African
itecture.

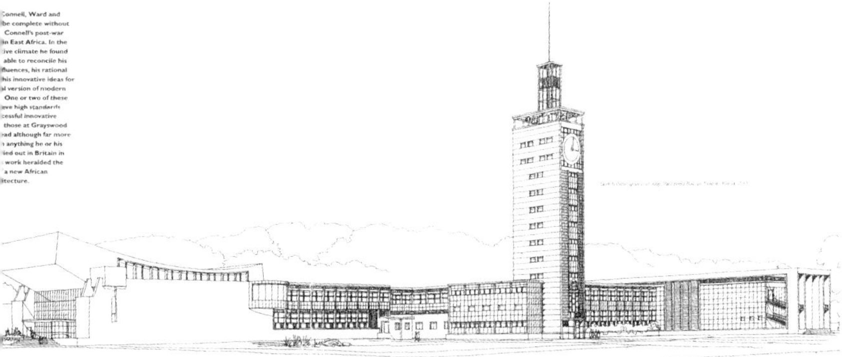

110 Aga Khan Awards for Architecture. Invitation and poster. London 1998.

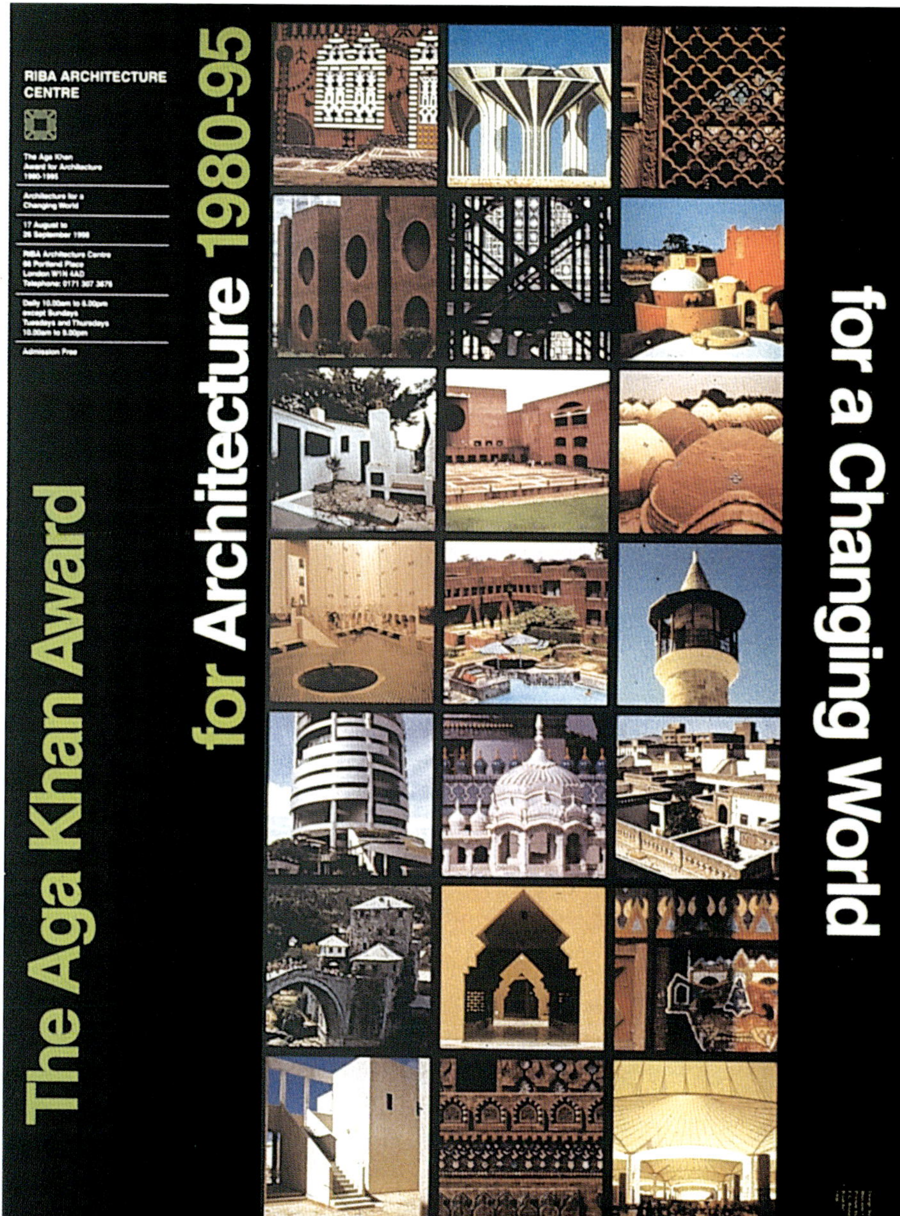

RIBA ARCHITECTURE
CENTRE
The Aga Khan
Award for Architecture
1980-1995
Architecture for a
Changing World
17 August to
RIBA Architecture Centre
66 Portland Place
London W1N 4AD
except Sundays
Tuesdays and Thursdays
Admission Free
The Aga Khan Award
for Architecture 1980-95
for a Changing World

 BookArt double-sided exhibition promotion. London 2000.

THE ARCHITECTURAL REVIEW

GARDENS

BRITISH
Book News
A38M Birmingham
A38 Lichfield
London (M1)
A monthly review of new books
Published by The British Council May 1985
Transport Studies 261 The National Book League 265

BRITISH
Book News
A monthly review of new books
Published by The British Council May 1986

BRITISH
Book News

BRITISH
Book News
A monthly review of new books
Published by The British Council August 1985

Newsletter. London 1996.

Architects Communicating Architecture

edited by Dennis Sharp

Association of Consultant Architects

Web Site
www.podproductions.co.uk/pod/aca

ACA | BOOK ART

Paul Davis & Partne

Sloane Square
London

Client
Cadogan Estates Group
Architects
Paul Davis & Partners
Structural Engineers
Adams Kara Taylor
Services Engineers
Transport Engineers
JMP Consultants Ltd
Quantity Surveyor

Paul Davis & Partners focus on contextual new buildings and conservation projects with an emphasis on mixed use and residential schemes.
The Sloane Square scheme highlights the intricacies of working in conservation areas and the need to balance renewal and redevelopment with the retention of existing facades. The project provides a revitalising mix of retail, residential and office uses as well as a newly …

5
Sloane Square Project, Model of proposals
6
Grosvenor Crescent Mews, Development of 13 mews houses, aerial photograph
7
Sloane Square Project
Perspective from Sloane Square
left
Computer generated view from Sloane Square showing tube tunnel

David Marks Julia Barfield Architects

Computer montaged illustrations of the British Airways Millennium Wheel (picture: Nick Wood/Hayes Davidson)

View from the top of the British Airways Millennium Wheel (photograph: Nick Wood)

British Airways Millennium Wheel Passenger Capsule (picture: [illegible])

British Airways Millennium Wheel Model (modelmakers: Andrew Ingham & Associates; photograph: Nick Wood)

David Marks Julia Barfield Architects is a young, award winning practice with a growing reputation for its innovative, environmentally aware and humanistic approach to architecture and design.
Operating from a large open-plan studio in London, David Marks Julia Barfield Architects are the originators and designers of the British Airways Millennium Wheel. Other projects on the drawing board include the Stoke Newington Reservoir in Hackney and the Weather-Watch Discovery Centre in Bracknell-one of the spearhead projects funded by the Millennium Commission.
Its Liverpool Watersports Centre received the 1995 Royal Institute of British Architects North West Award for Architecture and a Structural Steel Design Award 1995.

The British Airways Millennium Wheel is to be built over the River Thames opposite the Houses of Parliament. From the end of 1999, for a period of five years, millions of visitors will be able to enjoy unparalleled views over one of the world's most celebrated, historic and historically rich cities.
Described as London's answer to Paris's Eiffel Tower the 500 foot diameter Wheel will carry visitors in sixty high-quality enclosed passenger capsules for a spectacular 'flight' over the heart of the capital informing, educating and entertaining the public about London and its heritage. The highest observation wheel in the world, it will be a demonstration of the use of renewable energy, for example solar cells will be built into the passenger capsules and will help power the ventilation, lighting and communication systems.
The Wheel is a joint venture between British Airways and the Millennium Wheel Company. No public funds are being called for.

26 Architects Communicating Architecture

27 David Marks Julia Barfield Architects

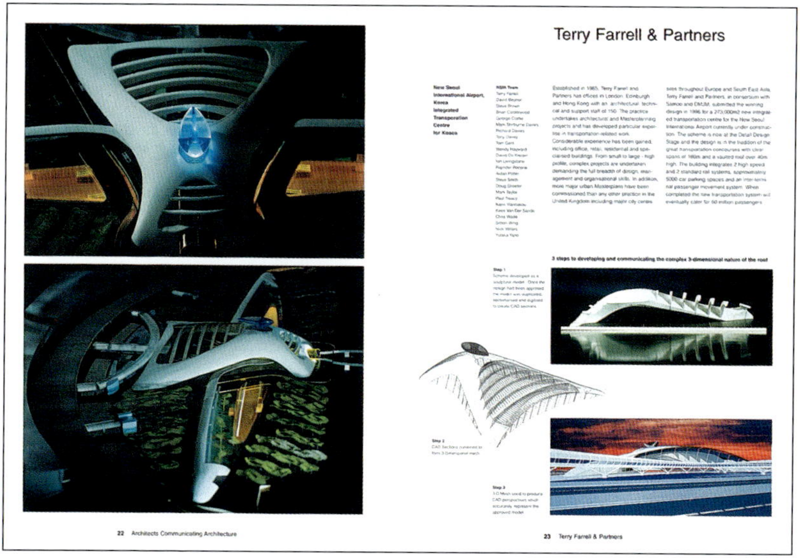

Terry Farrell & Partners

New Seoul International Airport, Korea Integrated Transporation Centre for Koaca

NSIA Team
Terry Farrell
David Beynon
Steve Brown
Brian Colclewood
George Coyne
Mark Sherburne Davies
Richard Davies
Tony Davey
Tom Gent
Wendy Hayward
David Di Kieper
Ian Livingstone
Rajinder Pooran
Aidan Potter
Steve Smith
Doug Streeter
Mark Taylor
Paul Tracey
Nami Wambakou
Kees Van Der Sande
Chris Wade
Simon Wing
Nick Willars
Yutaka Yano

Established in 1965, Terry Farrell and Partners has offices in London, Edinburgh and Hong Kong with an architectural, technical and support staff of 150. The practice undertakes architectural and Masterplanning projects and has developed particular expertise in transportation-related work.
Considerable experience has been gained, including office, retail, residential and specialised buildings. From small to large - high profile, complex projects are undertaken demanding the full breadth of design, management and organisational skills. In addition, more major urban Masterplans have been commissioned than any other practice in the United Kingdom including major city centres throughout Europe and South East Asia.
Terry Farrell and Partners, in consortium with Samoo and DMJM, submitted the winning design in 1996 for a 273,000m2 new integrated transportation centre for the New Seoul International Airport currently under construction. The scheme is now at the Detail Design Stage and the design is in the tradition of the great transportation concourses with clear spans of 160m and a vaulted roof over 40m high. The building integrates 2 high speed and 2 standard rail systems, approximately 5000 car parking spaces and an inter-terminal passenger movement system. When completed the new transportation system will eventually cater for 60 million passengers.

3 steps to developing and communicating the complex 3-dimensional nature of the roof

Step 1
Scheme developed as a sculptural model. Once the design had been approved the model was duplicated, sectionalised and digitised to create CAD sections.

Step 2
CAD Sections connected to form 3-Dimensional mesh.

Step 3
3-D Mesh used to produce CAD perspectives which accurately represent the approved model.

22 Architects Communicating Architecture

23 Terry Farrell & Partners

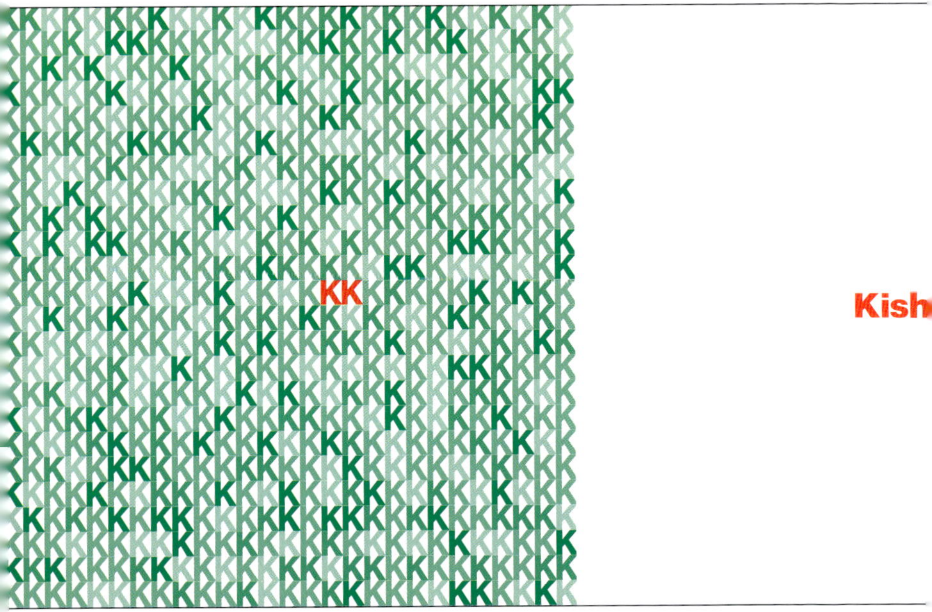

 Kisho Kurokawa. Kew Gardens. London 2002.

okawa

Design Brief
Barty Phillips
Number 1 Volume 2 April 1984

Design Brief
Barty Phillips
The May-fly.
NUMBER 2 VOLUME 2 MAY 1984

Building Centre Trust promotion. London 1996-2001.

 Chapman & Hall catalogue. London 1995.

The Building Centre
Maintenance Manual
+ Health and Safety File
Jacob Blacker
The Building Centre
Eminent Engineers
more
events@
buildingcentretrust.org
In Praise of Idleness. Ward
Atelier: 10 year retrospective.
events@
buildingcentretrust.org
SPORT
Sean Billings-
Billings Design Associates
28 February 6pm
The Building Centre Trust
education | design | construction
The Fabricators
Lecture series
Paul Rudolph—
American architect—
24 January - 19 February 2000
The Fabricators
Lecture series
Richard Brown
The Building Centre Trust
education | design | construction

20th Century Gallery

Ideas and information for teachers

'Tizio' desk lamp, Italy, 1973. (Circ. 505-1973)

V&A
Victoria and Albert Museum
20th CENTURY

Introduction

This booklet provides teachers with a brief introduction to the themes and objects in the 20th Century Gallery of the Victoria and Albert Museum, Rooms 70-74. It is designed to be used as a guide as teachers walk around the gallery planning a visit. The booklet also gives suggestions on preparing for a visit, activities to do in the gallery, and ideas to follow up back at school.

The 20th Century Gallery is arranged in chronological order beginning in Room 74 on Level B, which is up the stairs on the right as you enter through the Exhibition Road entrance. The gallery is divided into a number of rooms and bays, each covering a particular period. There are also cases devoted to lighting and radios in Room 74. Design Now, Room 70, presents changing displays on important design issues or the work of individual designers.

Fireplace designed by Charles Rennie Mackintosh, Britain, about 1904. Part of the furnishings for the Willow Tea Rooms, Glasgow, it combines Mackintosh's stylish ironwork with an industrially produced ceramic tile surround. (Circ. 244-1963)

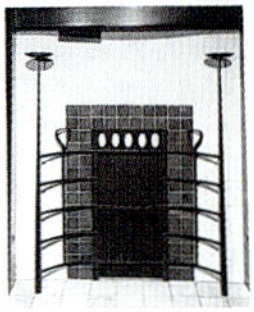

Stoneware vase, France, about 1928-30. The handpainted decoration combines African-inspired designs in brown/silver colouring with an abstract motif. (C.292-1987)

1900-1920

By 1900 mechanization was well established in manufacturing, but the question of its appropriate use was still fiercely debated. As factory production challenged traditional hand-manufacturing methods, designers and manufacturers responded in a number of ways.

Arts and Crafts attitudes
Goods made by craftsworkers were associated with high quality, and those with sufficient money could choose to own individually designed and handmade items. Many of the pieces shown in this case are explicitly handmade: books printed with specially cut type (no 8) and silverware with no mechanically cut or stamped decoration (nos 4,5,6). Although the overall aim of the Arts and Crafts movement was to improve design for everyone, the handmade item did not need to have mass appeal, as the desiger and maker were working for a clientele that wanted to express its good taste and individuality.

Commercial lines
Mechanization presented challenging opportunities for manufacturers. Some adapted craft items for production in great volume, or employed established designers to create pieces specifically for commercial production, such as printed tableware (no 37) and tablecloths (no 42). Stores like Liberty and Heal's stocked handmade pieces such as armchairs (no 39) though the bulk of their trade was in products made at least partially by machine. Liberty sold popular, inexpensive lines of machine-made furniture (nos 34, 35) that generally compared well with their handmade products.

Designers' responses to mechanization
As mechanization improved, designers and manufacturers explored its possibilities further, and began to use new materials. The 1906 furniture (no 51) is easy to assemble, an early forerunner of modern knockdown fittings, and uses aluminium for fixings as well as decoration. Iron mesh as used in the 1903 table (no 62) was starkly geometric and obviously machine-made. Plastic was used in the 1916 cabinet (no 59) for decoration only.

Manufacturers were busy adapting old products and creating new ones. The 1908 electric kettle (no 69) looks similar to traditional kettles, but with the protruding electrical socket as a small reminder of the new power source. The typewriter was a product that had no history, and so was not tied to any particular form. There is no attempt to hide the internal mechanisms of the 1916 portable model (no 52) as it was an office machine.

1920-1940

At this time, when there was a strong wish to leave the First World War far behind, designers and makers borrowed design themes from a number of different sources. Some attempted to capture the excitement of distant lands; others took their inspiration from the past.

Exoticism
For centuries new ideas have fed into the arts of the west through colonization and via trade routes. Increased international trade and the opening of more overseas markets meant that designers had fresh opportunities to use other countries and cultures as a source for design. As travel to foreign countries became more accessible, so romanticized 'exotic' styles came to symbolize wealth, worldliness and a sense of adventure, and reinforced imperial messages. Images such as palm trees, cacti and other non-native plant life were instantly recognizable as exotic. The vase with cover from about 1930 (no 22) is in the shape of a Chinese ginger jar and has Eastern-style decoration, but it is actually French. The 1924 biscuit tins designed to resemble ancient Egyptian vases (no 25) were part of a fashion fuelled by the discovery of Tutankhamun's tomb in 1922.

Surrealist art of the 1920s and '30s replaced the escapist appeal of distant lands with the fantasy of the subconscious. The 1936 couch designed by Salvador Dali (no 5), is a particularly striking piece of furniture because a pair of lips is put into such an unexpected context.

Exhibitions
Large national and international exhibitions were held in several countries during the 1920s and '30s. They were used by governments to promote national trade and manufacturing industries, and by designers to reach an international audience. Products shown at exhibitions often influenced subsequent design: the Brandt panel (no 23), which was first shown in Paris in 1925, led to further pieces being commissioned for the Selfridge's store in London in 1928.

Historicism
Designs from the past were often used to suggest learning, creativity and refinement, and were a comfortable reminder of tradition. The 1930 vase (no 37) shows that the ancient civilizations of Greece and Rome continued to be an important source of inspiration. A country's past designs could also be used to bolster national pride. British seventeenth- and eighteenth-century designs and techniques were revived on a range of British objects including wooden screens (no 38) and mugs (no 40). in France, pieces of furniture such as chairs and stools (no 36) and dressing tables (no 50) borrowed the ornate French Empire style, characteristic of the early nineteenth century.

 V & A Museum. London 1992.

Model B 32 chair designed by Marcel Breuer, Bauhaus, Germany, 1928. The natural beech and cane softened the new look of chrome-plated tubular steel and the revolutionary open cantilever frame. (W.10-1985)

...igners were bas-
...on the past and
...parallel school
...eaking with
...ghly influential
...ign movement
...lop objects but
...a rationale for
...tecture

...De Stijl
...desire to find the
...ugh art and
...pport for the
...hair designed by
...o 2) with its
...l planes, was
...hine production.
...ry simple to
...d. The seat and
...made in ply-
...s screwed to
...rts with pre-
...g dowel joints.

...haus art and
...lieved that
...ct came from
...hich form
...on. An 'honest'
...empt to hide its
...ction details or
...t it was made
...was to be inte-
...ials. The arm
...nufacturing
...using a new phi-
...n coupled with
...es like ergo-
...terials like tubu-
...st impact, and
...y original forms,
...r chair (no 10).
...ool taught a

wide range of courses on subjects from furniture and textiles to typography (nos 5-8), and metalwork (no 18; see also table lamps, lighting case, nos 6,11).

National traditions, tendencies and responses
Some designers adapted materials and forms to their own country's tastes and traditions. In Scandinavia designers did not reject past designs, but worked alongside the rapidly developing timber industry to develop plywood and laminated furniture. The 1930 armchair (no 40) looks quite different from Bauhaus design. In Britain, the Bauhaus school's most influential pieces were not universally popular, as the British did not take to metal in domestic interiors. The German designer Marcel Breuer, who pioneered metal furniture, worked in wood when designing in Britain (no 36).

The new style
As the new design look became accepted, designers concentrated more on symbolizing modern living and the future, and less on creating a new design philosophy. Images of speed and power were a constant source of inspiration. Smooth, streamlined shapes were often given to stationary objects like electric fan heaters (no 61) and radios (radio case, nos 5,13). Materials favoured by the Bauhaus, like glass and chromed metal, were combined decoratively with rare materials (no 70).

1900-NOW

Graphics for Communication
Mechanization brought changes to the printing industry and altered patterns of production and distribution. Mass communication developed alongside mass production as the range of household goods increased. Brand names, advertising and packaging became increasingly important (wallcase). The posters on the walls of the well area show how graphic design was used to sell products and services and as propaganda. The communication of information developed as a separate branch of graphics (wallcase and road sign on wall). Designers looked anew at letterforms, and experimented with typography, image and layout in books, leaflets and magazines (wallcase).

Polyprop Mark II chair, Britain, designed 1962-3. This was the first volume-produced injection-moulded polypropylene chair. It was cheap, light, easy to stack, and came with the matt grained texture on the seat already moulded on. Sales have passed 10 million. (Circ.15a-1968)

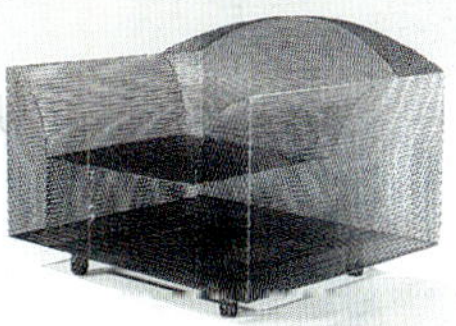

'How High the Moon' armchair, Switzerland, 1986-7. This chair was designed with sculptural qualities in mind and is more for looking at than for comfortable seating. Perforated zinc and steel. (W. 6-1990)

'Hebi' lamp, Italy, 1970. Metal and flexible plastic (Circ. 507-1976)

1945-1965

After the Second World War many western countries increased industrial output as a means of rebuilding their economies. Governments often promoted national design, and many companies saw innovative design as a means of increasing sales and making products appear desirable and unique.

Design and the state
Exhibitions were not the only means of state involvement in design. In Britain, the Utility scheme was introduced during the Second World War in an effort to control the price, quality and availability of some consumer goods, despite material and labour shortages. The designs of furnishings, clothing (no 17) and furniture (plinth), were standardized. Utility products such as the 1947 dressing table and 1950s chair were solid and well-made with little or no ornament. The scheme also raised awareness of approved design. Later, the 1951 Festival of Britain celebrated the anniversary of the Great Exhibition, and promoted its own style through products like wallpaper (no 2), plates (no 7) and carpets (no 16).

Popular choices
Developments in materials, manufacturing and marketing encouraged the emergence of new shapes and brighter colours. Fabrics made from artificial fibres (wallcase) and plastics like melamine (main case nos 6, 7), could imitate other materials and be made in bulk. The first polypropylene chair (plinth), had few parts, was easily contructed, and could be stacked for distribution and storage. From the consumer's viewpoint, plastic products were affordable, light, strong, durable and easy to clean.

New techniques also meant that new designs were possible. Mechanized screen printing enabled manufacturers to print cheaply a wide variety of patterns and colours on fabrics (wallcase) and industrial fastening methods were used in domestic storage units (plinth). The newness of consumer durables like the motor car was emphasized to the consumer through advertising (wallcase). As teenagers gradually developed real spending power, industry produced records (nos 23, 25), jewellery (no 24) and other goods aimed specifically at them.

Kettle made by Alessi, Italy, first produced in 1985. The smooth body looks less industrial with the addition of a brightly coloured handle, and an almost toy-like spout whistle. Stainless steel and polyamide. (M.11-b-1990)

1965-1990

The widespread availability of mass-produced goods caused some consumers to react against products that looked the same as everyone else's. Many designers tried to develop a design style that combined individuality with modern methods of production.

Style as statement
Objects do not exist just to perform a function; they can also suggest social aspirations. Everyday products like mugs (main case nos 15-21), T-shirts (wallcase), and badges (main case nos 30, 34-6) use images and slogans to make statements. Disposable items like paper dresses (main case nos 1, 2) reject traditional values of permanence and durability in favour of a throwaway culture. Things produced for the youth market are usually distinguished by the use of unconventional typography, strong colours and images (main case).

Italian partnerships
Post-war Italian designers have tried to combine elements of fun with sophistication in their work. Design groups like Memphis have produced highly decorated, eccentric objects that are quirky, but still part of mainstream design. Designs such as the 1983 Colorado teapot (no 6) and Murelia China radio, (radio case no 26) have taken ideas from cheap, mass-produced 1950s products, and used them to challenge conventional ideas on good form. European and Japanese manufacturers in the 1980s were sufficiently influenced to produce radios and personal hi-fi in 1950s style (radio case no 10).

Quotations and subversions
Design can be used to question the history of a product and our notions of the form it should take. The Bauhaus concentrated on the function of an object; some designers and makers have explored the very boundaries of what we understand an object to be. The 1984 teapot, (main case no 1) and tea and coffee sets, (main case no 10) are as much pieces of sculpture as they are functional objects. Books can break free of the printed page, and can explore the limits of narrative form, (main case nos 11,12,14,18). Almost anything can be transformed into jewellery - a fish head, for example, (no 13). Furniture can use shape or strange materials to create the unexpected (plinth).

1965-NOW

It is now possible for things to be made in various ways: singly or by the million, in workshops or factories, as craft objects or pieces of high technology. Even mass-produced items vary in the standards of precision, accuracy and finish. Consumers now are aware that the notion of 'quality' differs according to the product and its method of production.

Handmade: traditions
At the beginning of the century, things of high quality were almost exclusively handmade. Craft traditions still continue today, and handmade products like brogue shoes, (main case no 2) have come to symbolize care, skilled craftsmanship and respect for good materials. Items like the Paris chair (plinth) are one-off pieces, and emphasize the link between art and design. Though much skilled labour is used to produce them, there is still enough flexibility to cater to individual requirements.

Handmade: new art forms
The handmade object does not always refer back to tradition. Makers of ceramics, books, jewellery (main case and plinth) are creating artefacts that blur the dividing line between fine and applied arts. Their work often emphasizes an object's material quality and challenges its function.

Technology and design
Like craft producers, mass manufacturers have explored different ways of using new materials and

production technolo...
like the 1980 and 1...
(main case nos 5,6)...
trially produced bu...
made. The 1966 te...
(main case no 7), is...
with what appears...
painted lines, but is...
printed pattern. Ne...
can be used to rep...
without changing a...
the 1992 Dr Marte...
use the sole first d...
1947, but the uppe...
from polyester and...
that look like leathe...
technologies have...
obvious changes i...
The development ...
had a big impact o...
ign (no 1). Compute...
and manufacturing...
new graphic image...
(nos 9-12) and has...
textile production ...

Technology as a...
Early in the centur...
ogy came to symb...
and the future. Co...
tronic products suc...
(main case nos 2,3...
(main case no 5) a...
6,7) reveal their co...
emphasize high-te...
style. Miniaturizati...
sign of technologic...
seen in computers...
televisions (no 13),...
ers (no 14), calcula...
and telephones (n...
precision finish th...
achieved has led t...
for the matt black...
also lighting case ...

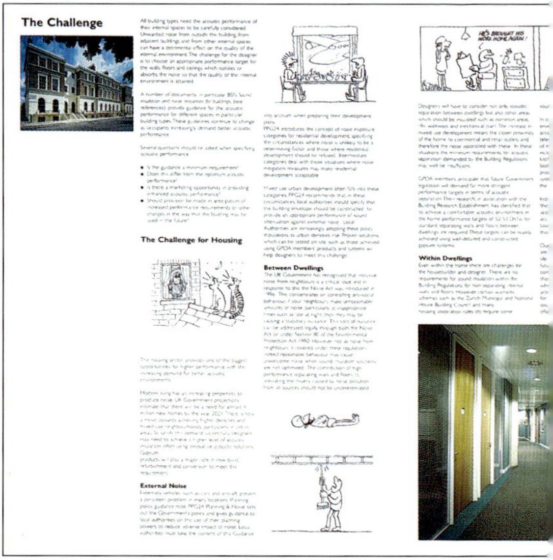

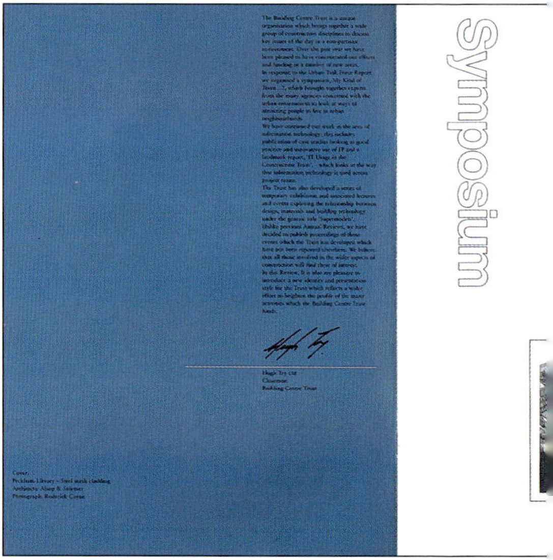

 The Building Centre Trust. London 2000.

The Working Environment

The trend toward providing open environments for better communication and productivity (which also demands a particular level of acoustic performance) has not diminished the need to provide spaces for meetings, consultations and places where people can work quietly or in private. Examples where this requirement is greater than normal are legal and medical workplaces.

The Selection of Appropriate Systems

Multiplex Cinema – Guildford

High performance plasterboard assembly

Multiplex Cinemas

Buildings for Music

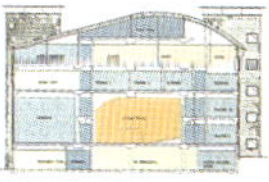

Leeds College of Music – Cross Section

Leeds College of Music

Architect: Building Design Partnership

The Selection of Appropriate Systems for Housing

Gypsum products provide the key to the achievement of excellent acoustic performance in housing. Solutions can be found for both new construction and upgrades of existing dwellings.

Masonry

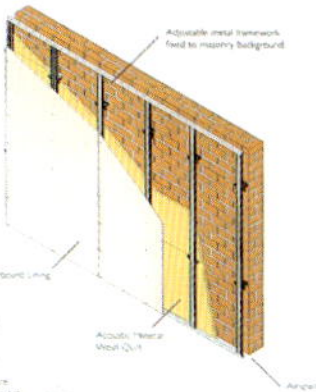

Frame Construction

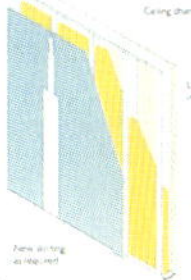

Lightweight non-loadbearing partition wall

Floors

Gypsum plasterboard as a component of a separating floor

My Kind of Town . . . ?
A consultative symposium on how to attract people to live in urban neighbourhoods

In 1999 the Urban Task Force report, Towards an Urban Renaissance, was published in response to the predicted demand for almost 4 million new homes in the UK over the next twenty-five years. In response to the Report the Building Centre Trust devised this symposium to build on the Urban Task Force recommendations for an urban renaissance, and put forward priorities and recommendations for the Government's Urban White Paper.

The symposium, which took place on 2 November 1999, was chaired by Will Hutton, then Editor in Chief of the Observer. The format of the event was a number of high-level discussion groups, involving 80 invited participants from a diversity of sectors. Brief introductory presentations were given on 'Developing Sustainable Urban Neighbourhoods' by David Rudlin, Northern Director of URBED, 'Marketing a New Urban Lifestyle' by Dr Michael Kelly, former Lord Provost of Glasgow, and 'Making an Urban Renaissance Financially Viable' by Yolande Barnes, Director of Research at FPDSavills. Discussion groups tackled a range of themes under the guidance of an expert convenor. Each table presented its recommendations to the plenary session where Dr Paul Evans, Head of Regeneration Directorate of the Department of the Environment, Transport and the Regions, gave an immediate response.

The presentations and discussion reports were recorded and an analysis of the ideas and conclusions collected are included in the 'My Kind of Town...' report. Participants provided examples of good practice that would together 'kick-start' a database of information for all those committed to an urban renaissance. Other participants' comments following the event and their particular perspectives of an urban renaissance and how it can be achieved are also included.

The resulting report presents the views of a select group from the design and construction industries and the wider field of urban regeneration. The report was presented to the DETR as part of consultation for the Government's Urban White Paper. It is presented in three parts. 'An urban renaissance would benefit all' sets out the case for focusing on urban regeneration in line with the dominant premise of the Urban Task Force's report. 'Achieving urban renaissance' includes the main conclusions from the symposium and the final part 'Urban renaissance is happening...' presents the case studies showing good practice.

The report is priced at £10.00 and is available from the Building Centre Trust.

Publications Information Technology

IT Case study

IT Case study

IT Case study

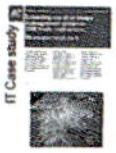

IT Case study

IT Usage in the Construction Team
A research report.

The Building Centre Trust has led and sponsored a number of Information Technology initiatives, most notably the publications Building IT2000 and Building IT2005 and a series of case studies promoting the benefits of Information Technology to the construction team.

Work on the case studies identified that instances of best practice across the disciplines in the design and construction processes are few. The extensive programme of research carried out for the report identified the extent to which the best practice experience is typical. The information it provides allows the exemplars from the current best practice projects to be effectively targeted to those with identified need, increasing the potential for realisation of the Egan Report's objectives through greater adoption of information technologies. Unlike most surveys the research was based around projects and not individual firms. This built up a much clearer picture of how IT is being used between the various disciplines and the progress towards standardised approaches.

It was found that construction industry organisations have invested heavily in both hardware and software, but there is still some way to go before this is integrated to the benefit of the project team.

The research was carried out by Lychgate Projects and was part-funded by the DETR under the Partners in Innovation Scheme as part of the IT Construction Best Practice Programme. It covers projects ranging in value from £1 million to over £30 million and looks at the impact of IT through such processes as document management, use of email and e-commerce.

'The integration of IT throughout the project team is the next big challenge for the industry' said John George, who chaired the project steering group. There is evidence that some headway has been made at some of the largest projects, but the benefits of an integrated approach to IT are less evident in projects of a smaller value. Why this should be was debated by an invited industry forum who had studied the findings of the research; the resulting messages from that forum are also included in the research report.

The report is a snapshot of current practice within the construction industry to help policy makers measure performance and target resources at appropriate initiatives. It will be of particular value to construction organisations, institutions and IT Service suppliers in their own policy making.

IT Usage in the Construction Team details by size and type of organisation and project:

- Organisational attitudes to IT
- Availability and use of IT tools
- Use of specialist construction software
- Recording and communicating information on projects
- Encouraging greater use of IT

The interpretation and conclusions of the industry forum include:

- Understanding the business benefits
- Construction e-commerce: an opportunity
- Interoperability
- Acceptability of electronic documents
- Awareness-raising and training.

The report costs £50.00 and is available from the Building Centre Trust.

The Building Centre Trust

Education | Design | Construction

The Building Centre Trust was established in 1963 as an independent charitable organisation to provide support for educational, research and cultural activities connected with the built environment. It occupies a central position, providing an opportunity for all sectors to work together for the benefit of the construction industry and those it serves.

The Trust derives its income from investments and from profits made by its wholly owned subsidiary The Building Centre. The Building Centre was established in 1931 and has been providing exhibition and information services to the profession and building component producers for nearly 70 years.

The Building Centre Trust
26 Store Street, London WC1E 7BT
Tel: 020 7692 6209 Fax: 020 7636 7149
www.buildingcentretrust.org

Registered Charity No 312833

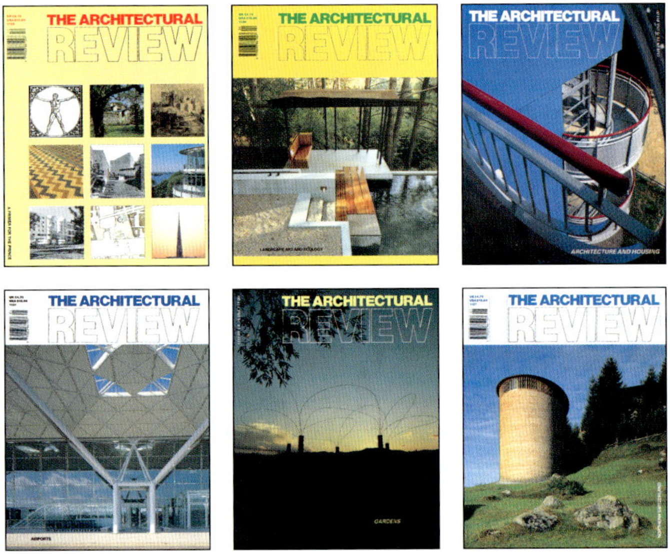

126 *The Architectural Review*. London 1989–1991.

Paris 200

Opéra

La Villette

La Défense

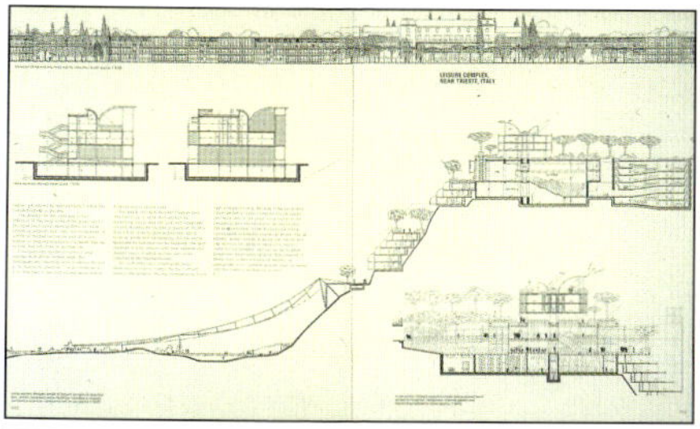
LEISURE COMPLEX,
NEAR TRIESTE, ITALY

Contrast

Place de Stalingrad

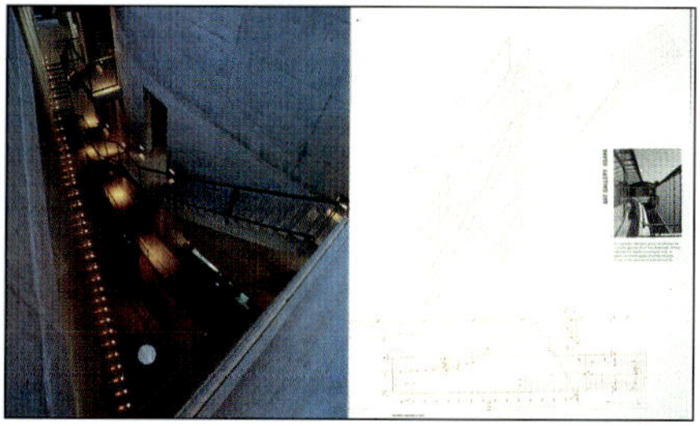

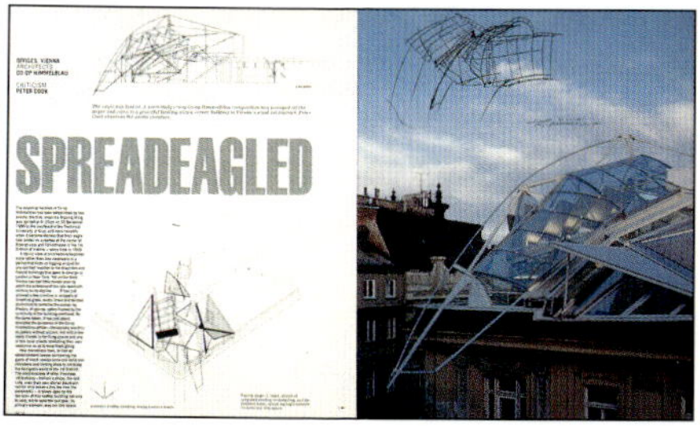
OFFICES, VIENNA
ARCHITECTS
CO OP HIMMELBLAU
CRITICISM
PETER COOK
SPREADEAGLED

NOUVEL
CUISINE

29.11.96